The Bridgestone
100 Best Places to Stay in Ireland

2012 EDITION

www.bridgestoneguides.com

THE BRIDGESTONE

100 BEST

PLACES TO STAY
IN IRELAND 2012

JOHN MCKENNA - SALLY MCKENNA

ESTRAGON PRESS

FIRST PUBLISHED IN JANUARY 2012

BY ESTRAGON PRESS

DURRUS

COUNTY CORK

© ESTRAGON PRESS

TEXT © JOHN & SALLY MCKENNA

THE MORAL RIGHT OF THE AUTHORS HAS BEEN ASSERTED

ISBN 978-1-906927-11-0

TYPESET IN GILL ALTERNATE AND SABON TO

AN ORIGINAL DESIGN BY NICK CANN

ILLUSTRATIONS BY AOIFE WASSER

PRINTED IN SPAIN BY GRAPHYCEMS

WRITTEN & EDITED BY JOHN MCKENNA

CONTRIBUTING EDITORS:

EAMON BARRETT

ORLA BRODERICK

CAROLINE BYRNE

ELIZABETH FIELD

CLAIRE GOODWILLIE

CAROLINE HENNESSY

CONNIE McKENNA

VALERIE O'CONNOR

JAKKI OWENS

LESLIE WILLIAMS

PUBLISHING EDITOR: SALLY MCKENNA

EDITOR: JUDITH CASEY

EDITORIAL ASSISTANT & WEB PICTURE EDITOR: EVE CLANCY

WEB: fluidedge.ie

FOR:

Ann Hamill

WITH SPECIAL THANKS TO

Des Collins, Colm Conyngham, Pat Curran,
Dr Denis Cotter, Grainne Byrne, Julie Barrett,
George Lane, Frank McKevitt, Margaret Deverell,
Lelia McKenna, Hugh Stancliffe, Eugene McSweeney,
Sam McKenna, PJ McKenna and
all our colleagues at Gill & Macmillan.

Bridgestone is the world's largest tyre and rubber company.

- Founded in Japan in 1931, it currently employs over 100,000 people in Europe, Asia and America and its products are sold in more than 150 countries. Its European plants are situated in France, Spain, Italy, Poland and Turkey.

- Bridgestone manufacture tyres for a wide variety of vehicles from passenger cars and motorcycles, trucks and buses to giant earthmovers and aircraft.

- Many new cars are fitted with Bridgestone tyres during manufacture, including Ford, Toyota, Volkswagen, Mercedes and BMW. Super cars such as Ferrari, Aston Martin and Porsche are also fitted with Bridgestone performance tyres as original equipment.

- Bridgestone commercial vehicle tyres enjoy a worldwide reputation for durability and its aircraft tyres are used by more than 100 airlines.
- Bridgestone tyres are distributed in Ireland by Bridgestone Ireland Ltd, a subsidiary of the multinational Bridgestone Corporation.

- A wide range of tyres is stocked in its 6,500 square metre central warehouse and its staff provide sales, technical and delivery services all over Ireland.

- Bridgestone tyres are available from First Stop Tyre Centres and tyre dealers throughout Ireland.

ECOPIa

- Bridgestone now offer a comprehensive range of low rolling resistance, fuel efficient tyres under the Ecopia brand name. These eco-friendly tyres are available in Ireland for both cars and commercial vehicles.

For further information:

BRIDGESTONE IRELAND LTD
10 Fingal Bay Business Park
Balbriggan
County Dublin

Tel: + 353 1 841 0000
Fax: + 353 1 841 5245

websites:
www.bridgestone.ie
www.firststop.ie
www.truckpoint.ie

• The most difficult job in the world isn't the lion tamer in the circus, or even the stand-up comedian in the seedy club. It isn't even the job of being Prime Minister of Greece. The hardest job in the world is, in fact, being a hotel manager.

• What makes the job so hard is not that you have to multi-task – many jobs require that – but the fact that you have to be able to do everything and oversee everything and then, ideally, you have to disappear. A hotel manager who is an overpowering presence in an hotel is a bad hotel manager: the good guys make sure everything works, but never let you see them doing it.

• So it's a delight in this newest edition of the *Bridgestone 100 Best Places to Stay in Ireland* to celebrate two hotel managers who have brought their hotels back into the *Bridgestone Guide*. Neil Grant in the West Cork Hotel in Skibbereen, and Dermot Madigan in The Mulranny Park Hotel in Mayo have brought great institutions back to acclaim and success. They have done it the only way there is to do it, via hard work, motivation, inspiration, dedication, and by working quietly and conscientiously. Of course, they both have great teams working with them. But hotels are like symphony orchestras: they need a great conductor in order to be great. Mr Grant and Mr Madigan are great conductors.

John & Sally McKenna
Durrus, West Cork, November 2011

"Eating is an intelligent act, or it's merely an animal one. And what makes it intelligent is the company of other mouths and minds. All animals eat. An animal that eats and thinks must think big about what it is eating not to be taken for an animal."

Adam Gopnik

• We need to think big about what we eat, as the writer Adam Gopnik advises in his book, *The Table Comes First.* Traditionally, thinking big about food meant thinking about complexity, about lavishness, about saturation. You thought big about what would end up on the plate, and not too much about where it came from, and how it got there in the first place.

• But to think big about food today, we need to see eating not merely as an intelligent act, but also, as Colin Sage points out in his book, *Environment and Food*, we need to see eating as an ecological act. How can you do this in an hotel, a B&B, a country house?

• Quite simply, you must source and serve the food of your place – your garden, your townland, your peninsula, your county. Ecology begins at home, and it begins with food ecology. It begins with thinking big about how the earth serves us, and how we can act to save it.

hot

classic

new

Something new

• The Bridgestone 100 Best Places to Stay in Ireland is arranged alphabetically by county, so it begins with County Carlow, which is followed by County Cavan, and so on. Within the counties, the entries are once again listed alphabetically. Entries in Northern Ireland are itemised alphabetically, at the end of the book. All NI prices are quoted in sterling.

• The contents of the Bridgestone 100 Best Guides are exclusively the result of the authors' deliberations. All meals and accommodation were paid for and any offers of discounts or gifts were refused.

• Many of the places featured in this book are only open during the summer, which means that they can be closed for any given length of time between October and March.

• **PRICES:** Average prices are calculated on the basis of one night's stay for bed and breakfast. Prices are subject to change, and therefore can only represent a guideline.

• **LISTINGS:** In every entry in the book we try to list telephone number, and internet details. We also request details of disabled access, the ability to cater for children, pets, plus any other relevant details.

• **GPS CO-ORDINATES:** We have printed co-ordinates as provided to us by the various establishments, written in Decimal Degrees Format. The *Bridgestone Guides*, however, can accept no responsibility for the ultimate accuracy of the co-ordinates provided to us.

• **TELEPHONE NUMBERS:** Telephone numbers are listed using the international dialling code. If you are calling a number within the country, omit the international code and use the 0.

• **BRIDGESTONE PLAQUES:** Look out for our Bridgestone Plaques, displayed by many of our listed establishments.

KILGRANEY COUNTRY HOUSE

Bryan Leech & Martin Marley
Bagenalstown
County Carlow
☎ **+353 (0) 59-977 5283**
🖰 **www.kilgraneyhouse.com**
✉ **info@kilgraneyhouse.com**

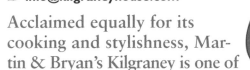

Acclaimed equally for its cooking and stylishness, Martin & Bryan's Kilgraney is one of the classic Irish country houses.

'It is a thoroughly modern country house hotel', wrote the great food writer Annie Bell, way back in 1999 when she first visited Bryan and Martin's Kilgraney House. 'The cooking,' said Ms Bell, 'sings with wonderfully clear notes'. Claire Goodwillie of the Bridgestone parish agrees: her most recent meal at Kilgraney won a single word of praise; 'wonderful'. Nowhere else is quite like Kilgraney, nowhere else has such a finely tuned aesthetic in every aspect of the operation, nowhere else has such ageless modernity, such feng shui. You have to applaud the fact that the house itself has changed little over the years, because they got it so right at the start that it hasn't needed to be tampered with. Vitally, Bryan Leech's cooking remains amongst the most intuitive and yet polished country house cooking you can enjoy anywhere. When you marry that smart cooking with the sense of style that blesses Kilgraney House, then you have a true Irish classic, a world-class Irish country destination.

● **OPEN:** Mar-Nov, Wed-Sun
● **ROOMS:** Six double rooms & two courtyard suites
● **PRICE: B&B** €85-€140 per person sharing. Midweek and aromatherapy packages available.

● **NOTES:** Visa, Mastercard, Amex, Laser. Dinner, 8pm, €52 (Six course), book by noon. Wheelchair access with assistance, please phone to discuss needs. Aroma Spa. Children over 12 only.

● **DIRECTIONS:**
Just off the R705, 6km from Bagenalstown.
GPS 52.653333 -6.957222

STEP HOUSE HOTEL

James & Cait Coady
Main Street, Borris
County Carlow
📞 **+353 (0) 59-977 1624**
🖱 **www.stephousehotel.ie**
📧 **info@stephousehotel.ie**

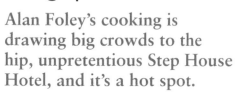

Alan Foley's cooking is drawing big crowds to the hip, unpretentious Step House Hotel, and it's a hot spot.

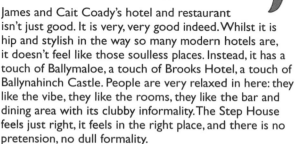

James and Cait Coady's hotel and restaurant isn't just good. It is very, very good indeed. Whilst it is hip and stylish in the way so many modern hotels are, it doesn't feel like those soulless places. Instead, it has a touch of Ballymaloe, a touch of Brooks Hotel, a touch of Ballynahinch Castle. People are very relaxed in here: they like the vibe, they like the rooms, they like the bar and dining area with its clubby informality. The Step House feels just right, it feels in the right place, and there is no pretension, no dull formality.

And the cooking is wow! Chef Alan Foley uses superb local artisan foods and knows just what to do with them. Our main course of Carlow free-range chicken where the breast had been roasted, the leg confited, was served with a little foie gras, a celeriac purée and a tarragon jus, and was simply perfect, though the sheer perfection of the homemade taglioni served with Kilmore scallops was actually one of the outstanding pieces of cooking of 2011. The Step House is hot!

● **OPEN:** All year
● **ROOMS:** 20 bedrooms
● **PRICE:** B&B from €65-€85 per person sharing. Single supplement €10

● **NOTES:** Visa, Mastercard, Laser. Full wheelchair access. 1808 Bar lunch & dinner, 12.20pm-2pm, 6pm-9.30pm. Rubens Restaurant opens Fri & Sat, 6pm-9pm

● **DIRECTIONS:**
Borris is in between Carlow and Kilkenny, and the hotel is on the main street in the village.
GPS 52.601244 -6.927553

MacNEAN TOWNHOUSE

Neven & Amelda Maguire
Blacklion
County Cavan

📞 **+353 (0) 71-985 3022**
🖱 **www.macneanrestaurant.com**
✉ **info@macneanrestaurant.com**

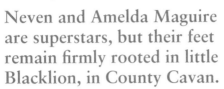

Neven and Amelda Maguire
are superstars, but their feet
remain firmly rooted in little
Blacklion, in County Cavan.

Here is the good news: the MacNean Townhouse has extended. There are now 17 rooms adjoin-
ing the restaurant, so getting a bed and a table is now
almost within the reach of mere mortals. So, start to
plan that trip to Neven and Amelda Maguire's restaurant
with rooms in little Blacklion, County Cavan. And if you
make the pilgrimage to come to Blacklion, then what will
you find when you arrive? A modest, unassuming house
in the most modest, unassuming village. You will, quite
frankly, be astonished: this world-famous restaurant in
this wee hamlet!? Really!? Well, yes, actually.
This is the way in which the Maguires have turned the
world on its head: traditionally, chefs and hoteliers have
gone out to find their audience. But, with the MacNean,
the audience comes to them and for simple reasons: the
cooking and the hospitality here are world-class, and
they are both linked to the place, inextricably. So, you
have to experience them in situ: Cavan food, and Cavan
hospitality.

● **OPEN:** All year, except January
● **ROOMS:** Seventeen rooms
● **PRICE:** B&B €67-€96 per person sharing

● **NOTES:** Visa, Mastercard, Laser. MacNean Restaurant open 6pm-9.30pm Wed-Sat; 1pm & 3.30pm, 7pm-
8.30pm Sun (closed Wed low season). Sun Lunch €39,
Dinner €67-€82.
Recommended for vegetarians.

● **DIRECTIONS:**
On the main street in Blacklion.
GPS 54.291361 -7.877739

THE OLDE POST INN

Tara McCann & Gearoid Lynch
Cloverhill, Butler's Bridge
County Cavan
☎ **+353 (0) 47-55555**
🖱 **www.theoldepostinn.com**
✉ **gearoidlynch@eircom.net**

One of the jewels of the borderlands, Tara and Gearoid's Olde Post Inn is a special place to stay, run by a smart, quietly subversive pair of hosts.

Great chefs have always been subversive of mainstream culture, and Gearoid Lynch is no exception. As commissioner-general of Eurotoques Ireland, Mr Lynch presented one of the annual Eurotoques awards in October 2011 to David Tiernan, maker of one of Ireland's finest cheeses, Glebe Brethan, and seller of raw milk. The Government plans to ban the sale of raw milk. At the presentation of the awards, bottles of Mr Tiernan's raw milk had to be removed before the photoshoot could take place with the Minister. *The Irish Times* reported that Mr Lynch also said 'Seventy five percent of what I cook now comes from within a 10-mile range of the restaurant'. So, Mr Lynch is not merely a political subversive, he is also a local champion, and it is these factors that make The Olde Post so special. It's a wonderful place to stay with wonderful cooking, with a true sense of the culture of County Cavan and of the borderlands and of all the riches of this place. And Tara and Gearoid are as smart as it gets, and as subversive.

● **OPEN:** all year, except Christmas
● **ROOMS:** Six double rooms.
● **PRICE:** B&B €100 per double room

● **NOTES:** Olde Post Inn restaurant open 6pm-9pm Tue-Thu, 6pm-9.30pm Fri-Sat, 12.30pm-2.30pm, 5.30pm-8.30pm Sun. Dinner €54, Sun Lunch €33. No wheelchair access.

● **DIRECTIONS:**
From Cavan follow N3. At Butler's Bridge, take the N54 and the Olde Post is 3km further, on the right. GPS 54.0801 -7.3701

CULLINAN'S

James & Carol Cullinan
Doolin
County Clare
📱 **+ 353 (0) 65-707 4183**
🖥 **www.cullinansdoolin.com**
📧 **cullinans@eircom.net**

Highly professional and highly personal, James & Carol's restaurant with rooms seems to breathe the very spirit of nimble, artful, busy, darling Doolin.

James and Carol Cullinan's excellent restaurant with rooms in the centre of Doolin is a peachy, professional destination. What is particularly nice about the newer rooms at Cullinan's is their proximity to the river, views of which can be enjoyed from their balconies, and whilst the rooms are compact, floor-to-ceiling glass walls have the clever effect of making them seem huge. They are chic and stylish getaways, and both the bedrooms and the public rooms enjoy superlative housekeeping, so Cullinan's gleams.

James Cullinan's cooking is based on classic principles and techniques, allied to good sourcing of his ingredients. It's a template that has served him unshakably over the years whilst also keeping his food up to date in dishes such as sea bream with a smoked salmon and spring onion risotto, or marinated Burren lamb with a spring roll filled with confit shank of lamb, and in good puddings like baked caramel cheesecake. Excellent breakfasts will set you up for that promising day ahead.

- **OPEN:** mid Feb-mid Dec
- **ROOMS:** Ten double & twin rooms
- **PRICE:** B&B €32.50-€50 per person sharing, €40-€70 single

- **NOTES:**
Visa, Mastercard, Laser. No wheelchair access.
Restaurant open 6pm-9pm (closed Wed & Sun), dinner €30-€45

- **DIRECTIONS:**
At the crossroads, coming down from the school, in centre of Doolin. GPS N+53°0'59.03" W-9°22'38.37"

GREGAN'S CASTLE

Simon Haden & Frederieke McMurray
Ballyvaughan
County Clare
📞 + 353 (0) 65 707 7005
🖰 www.gregans.ie
📧 stay@gregans.ie

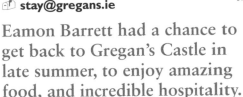

Eamon Barrett had a chance to get back to Gregan's Castle in late summer, to enjoy amazing food, and incredible hospitality.

Back again in Gregan's Castle for a few days r'n'r in late summer 2011, Eamon Barrett reflects on what Simon, Freddie and Mickael have achieved in this extraordinary place to stay:

'I suppose from an accommodation point of view there is not much I can say except this: I hope I'll be holidaying here for the rest of my life. There are only a handful of places in the country – Longueville House, Richmond House and Ballyvolane House come to mind – that manage to achieve the level of relaxation that one feels as a guest at Gregan's Castle. That magic formula of The Property + The People = Hospitality may seem simple but it's as elusive as properly cooked scrambled egg. At Gregan's, that hospitality seems as natural to the staff as breathing. What lifts Gregan's into the stratosphere is the extraordinary cooking of Mickael Viljanen and his team.'

The stratosphere is right: Gregan's has transcended mortal coils: it's way, way out there, out on its own.

- **OPEN:** 10 Feb-24 November
- **ROOMS:** 21 rooms and suites
- **PRICE:** €160-€325 per room

- **NOTES:** Restaurant open 6pm-9pm Mon-Sat, €69. Seasonal Sunday menu served in dining room, 1pm-7pm. Bar lunch 12.30pm-2pm Mon-Sat. Burren tours arranged. Wheelchair access. Croquet lawn.

- **DIRECTIONS:**
3.5 miles outside Ballyvaughan village.
GPS 53.076944 -9.186222

10 PLACES TO

TAKE A BATH

1

BALLYVOLANE HOUSE
COUNTY CORK

2

CLIFF HOUSE HOTEL
COUNTY WATERFORD

3

COOPERSHILL HOUSE
COUNTY SLIGO

4

EMLAGH HOUSE
COUNTY KERRY

5

INIS MEÁIN SUITES
COUNTY GALWAY

6

MOORFIELD LODGE
COUNTY DONEGAL

7

MOY HOUSE
COUNTY CLARE

8

NEWTOWN HOUSE
COUNTY CORK

9

QC'S
COUNTY KERRY

10

THE ROSS
COUNTY KERRY

MORRISSEY'S

Hugh Morrissey
Doonbeg
County Clare

☎ +353 (0) 65-905 5304
🖰 www.morrisseysdoonbeg.com
✉ info@morrisseysdoonbeg.com

Terrific value, for both excellent cooking and splendid rooms, makes Morrissey's riverside 'dinner'n'duvet' your favourite south Clare address.

Hugh Morrissey has transformed this lovely pub from a traditional Irish bar into a svelte restaurant with rooms, yet he has somehow managed to keep the graceful ambience of the old place, where four generations of the Morrissey family have plied their trade. The cooking is modern and informal – chicken Caesar salad; Angus beef burger; salmon and cod fish cake; home-made scampi with tartare sauce – food that you can relax with. That relaxed air is worth dwelling on, for it's really the signature of Morrissey's, a destination that enjoys a youthful, laid-back sang-froid that is hard to resist. We have remarked before on the incredible feat that Hugh Morrissey has performed in his stylish 'dinner'n'duvet', transforming it from a simple family-run pub that was open for only a few months of the year into a dynamic 'D'n'D' that now opens fully for ten months of the year. Another excellent restaurant with rooms, the sort of thing they do with style, creativity and panache here in the Banner County.

● **OPEN:** March-Dec
● **ROOMS:** Seven rooms
● **PRICE:** B&B €90 per room, €50 single

● **NOTES:** Visa, Mastercard, Laser, Amex. Pub restaurant opens for lunch, 12.30pm-2.30pm, and dinner, 6pm-9.30pm, €35. (Closed Sun evening)

● **DIRECTIONS:**
From Ennis, follow the Kilrush road. In Kilrush follow signs for Kilkee, and then look for the Doonbeg sign. The pub is right beside the bridge in the centre of the village. GPS 52.730861 -9.524353

MOUNT VERNON

Ally Raftery & Mark Helmore
Flaggy Shore, New Quay,
Burren, County Clare

📞 **+353 (0) 65-707 8126**
🖱 **www.mountvernon.ie**
✉ **info@mountvernon.ie**

How long did it take
Connie McKenna to fall in
love with Mount Vernon?
How fast is a nano-second?

'Mount Vernon is a house of true beauty', says Connie McKenna. One of its secrets is that it shows the importance of travel, as everywhere you look an artefact collected from Asia, Africa, South America, or elsewhere is to be found in exactly the right place within the room. Yet it's not cluttered, it's almost as if all the ornaments ran into the house and chose their own space. Paintings and concave mirrors are scattered across the walls. The living room, in particular, is a place where you can find your heart in true comfort. The food is simply delightful: fish broth with prawns, lemon and dill nourishes the soul inside out. Halibut, juicy to the bone and well cooked, with new potatoes and colourful, well-cooked vegetables. This is what simple, honest, home cooking is about. To top things up beautifully, Ally's homemade apple pie was country cooking at its most delightful: every mouthful took our palates on a journey. Mount Vernon fits beautifully with the wild Flaggy Shore – Ally and Mark have made a special place here.

● **OPEN:** April 1-Oct 31, or by arrangement
● **ROOMS:** Five rooms, all en suite or with private bathroom
● **PRICE:** B&B €90-€115 per person sharing. €30 single supplement

● **NOTES:** Visa, Mastercard, Laser, Amex. Guided walks and fishing can be arranged.

● **DIRECTIONS:**
Signposted at two points from the main Ballyvaughan-Kinvara Road.
GPS 53.155, -9.080

MOY HOUSE

Antoin O'Looney (owner)
Brid O'Meara (General Manager)
Lahinch, County Clare
☎ **+353 (0) 65-708 2800**
🖰 **www.moyhouse.com**
✉ **bomeara@moyhouse.com**

Brid O'Meara is a dynamic personality who exudes hospitality, and the singular and striking Moy House benefits from her drive and determination.

Moy House is the real deal. It's handsome, it's distinctive, it's singular. It's a house that unwinds its charms slowly, a quiet, seductive destination that soon captivates you. Here is Eamon Barrett on his visit to Brid O'Meara's house: 'Initially I wasn't sure I liked it. But the more time I spent there, reading, looking out to the rough sea, helping myself to Power's 12-year-old whiskey from the honesty bar, the more I liked it. We had a beautiful room with a built-in window seat and a fabulous bathroom. Lorge chocolates from West Cork were left in the room for us. In the evening, there were slippers and candles lighting. We had our own turf fire in the room, for goodness sake! At breakfast the next morning there was a taste of the level that Moy is pitched at, with truly superb service and an excellent breakfast of scrambled egg with mushroom accompanied by really good brown bread. Staff were excellent - again that all-important welcome from Brid - and nothing we asked for was too much trouble.'

● **OPEN:** Mar-Dec
● **ROOMS:** Nine rooms
● **PRICE:** B&B €185-€280 per double room, Suite €270-€360, Single €145-€175

● **NOTES:**
Visa, Mastercard, Laser. Special offers Nov-May. Special packages/group rates available. Dinner, €55.

● **DIRECTIONS:**
Moy House is located about 1.5km south of Lahinch town, on the Miltown Malbay road. Shannon Airport is 45 mins drive. GPS 52.951381 -9.346285

SHEEDY'S

John & Martina Sheedy
Lisdoonvarna
County Clare
+353 (0) 65-707 4026
www.sheedys.com
info@sheedys.com

north
east
west
south

Sheedy's is one of the bestest, nicest family-run hotels in Ireland. Happily for us all, it's as fine today in the present as it has been for generations.

Sheedy's is one of those discreet, modest, family-run hotels that once expressed the hospitality culture of Ireland, and, happily, that meticulous, subtle and charming culture of Irish hospitality lives on in this family hotel, thanks to Martina Sheedy's polite, quiet service, and John Sheedy's utterly delicious cooking.

Everything here is done by hand, from the handcrafted work of their brilliant local suppliers to the hands-on care of the kitchen. Sheedy's does things the old-fashioned way. 'All dishes are cooked fresh to order', it says at the foot of their dinner menu, which also describes their dedicated local suppliers, and that cooked-to-order care extends to breakfast, every part of which is cooked individually and served by the team. John and Martina Sheedy have to work hard to do this intensive hands-on hospitality, and it is the happy guest who benefits in this pretty and simple hotel. Simple it may be, but its heart is the very heart of hospitality, the essence of Irish generosity, and simple deliciousness.

● **OPEN:** from Easter to early October
● **ROOMS:** Eight rooms and three junior suites
● **PRICE:** €99-€170 per room

● **NOTES:** All major cards accepted.
One room wheelchair accessible.
Restaurant open during summer, and ring off season.
Special offers available all year, telephone for details.

● **DIRECTIONS:**
200m from the centre of Lisdoonvarna, on the road going out towards the wells.
GPS 53.02771 -9.28909

VAUGHAN LODGE

Michael & Maria Vaughan
Lahinch
County Clare

🕯 **+353 (0) 65-708 1111**
🔗 **www.vaughanlodge.ie**
✉️ **info@vaughanlodge.ie**

The Vaughan dynasty has practised
the art of hospitality in Lahinch for
generations now, and Michael and
Maria continue the noble tradition.

Multi-millionaire Chip O'Hare stayed at Vaughan Lodge
as part of a golfing trip with a bunch of similarly affluent
buddies during the summer of 2011. Kathy Sheridan of
The Irish Times asked Chip what he reckoned of Michael
and Maria Vaughan's handsome lodgings: 'Vaughan Lodge
was excellent', wrote Chip. 'Obviously new and neat and
clean. Superb food and service was cordial and first rate.
Michael was a great host and hard worker. We had a dinner there on our last night with the guys from Lahinch
and it was lovely.'
Well, that's the million-dollar American market taken
care of for the foreseeable future, and if you had to bet
on a guy to convince those choosy Yanks, then Michael
Vaughan would be your banker. He is a consummate
professional, which makes Vaughan's a wonderful place to
stay and to eat. Kathy Sheridan also described the sheer
effort and dedication it takes from the Vaughans to run a
place like this: you know it ain't easy, even if they make it
look easy. That's what professionals do.

● **OPEN:** Apr-Nov
● **ROOMS:** 20 rooms, all en suite
● **PRICE:** €85-€135 per person sharing.
Single €95-€160

● **NOTES:** All major cards accepted. Full wheelchair
access. Restaurant, dinner €47. Open 6.30pm-9.15pm
Tue-Sat. Private car parking. Loc8 code K20-7303MF

● **DIRECTIONS:**
From Ennis, take the N85 to Ennistymon, turn left onto
N67 to Lahinch, and the hotel is just inside the 50km
zone on the left. GPS 52.933889 -9.341111

WILD HONEY INN

Aidan McGrath & Kate Sweeney
Kincora Road, Lisdoonvarna
County Clare
📞 **+353 (0) 65-707 4300**
🖥 **www.wildhoneyinn.com**
✉ **info@wildhoneyinn.com**

A charming inn with spiffing cooking, Aidan McGrath & Kate Sweeney have a delightful place.

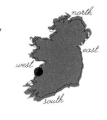

Something new

'Just like Vaughan's in Liscannor, The Wild Honey Inn confounds your expectations by placing really stellar cooking at the centre of its USP', says Eamon Barrett. 'The hotel exterior is certainly pleasant but gives no clue that the food served inside will be anything other than standard hotel fare. But standard hotel fare it ain't: a starter of gravadlax is really good, that lovely clean taste that comes from delicately cured fish is just perfect, especially when served with some really good brown bread. A rare rib-eye steak with twice-cooked chips is served with salsa verde, again perfect cooking. Service throughout is understated and genuine and a real sense of care permeates.' Too right, Eamon. John McKenna also made it to the WHI, and was particularly amazed by the brilliant breakfasts, which utilise the products of great local specialists to deliver a knock-out of fantastic tastes and textures. You can even get an omelette Arnold Bennett for breakfast here, one of the great treats in the West. The Wild Honey is ace.

● **OPEN:** mid Feb-end Dec, with restricted hours off season
● **ROOMS:** 14 rooms, all en suite
● **PRICE:** €40 per person sharing.

● **NOTES:** Visa, Mastercard, Laser. Wheelchair access. Restaurant, open 1pm-3.30pm, 5pm-9pm during the summer

● **DIRECTIONS:**
From Ennis, take the N18 to Ennistymon. Take the N67 towards Lisdoonvarna, Inn is on your right at the edge of town.

ASHLEE LODGE

Anne & John O'Leary
Tower, Blarney
County Cork
☎ **+353 (0) 21-438 5346**
🖰 **www.ashleelodge.com**
🖂 **info@ashleelodge.com**

Anne and John's Ashlee Lodge is your home from home when visiting beautiful Blarney. But if only home was as comfortable as lovely Ashlee Lodge.

Anne and John O'Leary describe Ashlee as a four-star private hotel, but one of the secrets of their house is the fact that it doesn't feel anything like a conventional hotel, and it doesn't look like an hotel, though it does enjoy hotel levels of decor and comfort.

But what no other comparable four-star hotel could offer is the incomparable service that this dedicated couple practice. Nothing is too much of a problem for these splendid people, and the O'Learys even seem, at times, to be mind-readers, capable of knowing what it is you need, or might need, or might like, or would like, even before you articulate the request yourself.

Their care extends to every detail of Ashlee – the superb cooking they offer, enjoyed in the warming, bright conservatory; the level of comfort in public and private rooms; the cosy drawing room with its honour bar. Above all, there is the constant presence of Anne and John themselves, as they prove themselves masters of the art of hospitality in each and every detail of Ashlee.

● **OPEN:** 20 Jan-20 Dec
● **ROOMS:** 10 rooms, all en suite, made up of six executive rooms, two mini suites and two master suites
● **PRICE:** €89 for standard room, €120 for mini suite, €180 for master suite, per person sharing

● **NOTES:** All major cards accepted. Dinner Tue-Sat, €45. Wheelchair access. No facilities for children. Secure parking. Pet friendly. Outdoor hot tub.

● **DIRECTIONS:**
From Blarney, take the R617 for 1.5km to Tower.
GPS 51.924328 -8.612233

BALLYMALOE HOUSE

The Allen family
Shanagarry, Midleton
East Cork

📞 **+353 (0) 21-465 2531**
🖱 **www.ballymaloe.com**
✉ **res@ballymaloe.ie**

The Allen family's Ballymaloe House represents an ideal
Ireland: modest, charming,
pastoral, lovely.

Ballymaloe House is a bit like what people say about
The Irish Times: other destinations exist to make money,
but Ballymaloe makes money in order to exist. It's a
profound difference, and it goes a long way to explain-
ing the unique, ageless charm and character of Ireland's
most famous address. With the Grain Store hosting
excellent concerts of all styles, and new farm cottages
and apartments created out in the yard, Ballymaloe is
slowly, organically extending beyond the original family
home where guests traditionally stay. But whether you
want to do some self-catering, or enjoy all the aspects
of the house by staying as a guest, the fact remains
that Ballymaloe's star remains undimmed after almost
half-a-century of hospitality. The Allen family quietly and
modestly go about their business, which is, frankly, to be
the best in the business. New family members arrive and
contribute their skills and gifts to this mighty enterprise.
The cooking is as fine as ever, the service understated.
There is nowhere else in the world like it.

● **OPEN:** All year, apart from Christmas & 2 weeks in Jan.
● **ROOMS:** 30 rooms. No suites
● **PRICE:** B&B €80-€125 per person sharing. Single
€105-€124

● **NOTES:** All major cards accepted. Dinner 7pm-
9.30pm, €70 (buffet dinner on Sun night, 7.30pm).
Recommended for vegetarians. Children welcome, early
dinner. Parking. Two wheelchair-friendly bedrooms.

● **DIRECTIONS:**
From Cork take N25 to exit for Whitegate R630, follow
signs for R629. GPS -8.074930 W 51.865310 N

BALLYVOLANE HOUSE

Justin & Jenny Green
Castlelyons, Fermoy
North Cork
📞 **+353 (0) 25-36349**
🖰 **www.ballyvolanehouse.ie**
✉ **info@ballyvolanehouse.ie**

Justin and Jenny's Ballyvolane
House has, above all its many
charms, the most perfect
country ambience.

'For my money, one of THE stellar country houses, and
In the ascendant.' Our editor Eamon Barrett's summa-
tion of Ballyvolane House was ecstatic, but Eamon's
reaction is no more than what every guest who stays at
this most beautiful house finds themselves saying when
it is time to leave, time to say goodbye to Justin and
Jenny, time to return to reality. How do they do it? How
do they weave this spell? Time and again at this house
we have seen people succumb, almost as if they were
hypnotised in some way.
Quite simply, Mr and Mrs Green understand exactly
how to give a destination just exactly the feeling, the ambience, the fiction, the dream, that you want the house
to have. This means that Ballyvolane feels exactly the way
you want a country house to feel: timeless, pristine, cul-
tured, sheerly beautiful, welcoming, hospitable, friendly,
out of time. Ballyvolane House is quite simply superb,
and offers one of the greatest country house experiences you can enjoy anywhere.

● **OPEN:** 1 Jan-23 Dec
● **ROOMS:** Six rooms, all en suite
● **PRICE:** B&B €75-€105 per person sharing. Single
€120-€125

● **NOTES:** Visa, Mastercard, Laser, Amex. Dinner 8pm,
€50, communal table. Private car park. Children welcome. Self catering also available. Pet friendly.

● **DIRECTIONS:**
From the N8, south just after Rathcormac, take the turn
to Midleton and look for the sign for the house.
GPS 51.096822 -7.530917

BLINDGATE HOUSE

Maeve Coakley
Blindgate, Kinsale
West Cork

📞 **+353 (0) 21-477 7858**
🖱 **www.blindgatehouse.com**
✉ **info@blindgatehouse.com**

Maeve Coakley's pretty house is a great address in Kinsale, with a perfect location in the quiet end of town, lovely cooking, and fabulous style.

We have always loved the style of Maeve Coakley's house, and the fact that its rather conventional exterior hides one of the most superbly designed and executed interiors of any house in this entire book.
But style doesn't win out over comfort in Blindgate, and so this is a very cosy house to hang out in, and not one of those design traps that involves you suffering for someone else's art. As such, Blindgate is a terrific base for staying, relaxing and exploring, enjoying all the best of Kinsale whilst just being far enough up the hill to ensure peace and quiet when the town is at full tilt, but also allowing you to head out both eastwards and westwards through County Cork to sample the incredible varieties of the county, both geographically and gastronomically. Breakfasts are just as stylish and fine as the design, setting you up for the perfect day. The designer John Rocha operates by the maxim that 'If you get the design right at the start, you don't need to change it later'. Blindgate shows how to do just that.

● **OPEN:** Mar-Dec
● **ROOMS:** 11 rooms (seven twin rooms, three standard double rooms & one superior double)
● **PRICE:** B&B €100-€160 per room

● **NOTES:** Visa, Mastercard, Amex. No dinner. Wheelchair access with assistance, but no walk-in showers. Enclosed parking.

● **DIRECTIONS:**
200m past St Multose Church – just up the hill from the Kinsale Gourmet Store.
GPS 51.703842 -8.5253852

FORTVIEW HOUSE

Violet O'Connell
Gurtyowen, Toormore
Goleen, West Cork
📱 **+353 (0) 28-35324**
🖱 **www.fortviewhousegoleen.com**
📧 **fortviewhousegoleen@eircom.net**

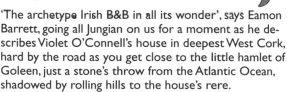

'Probably the best B&B we have ever stayed in', says Eamon Barrett of the *Bridgestone Guides.*

'The archetype Irish B&B in all its wonder', says Eamon Barrett, going all Jungian on us for a moment as he describes Violet O'Connell's house in deepest West Cork, hard by the road as you get close to the little hamlet of Goleen, just a stone's throw from the Atlantic Ocean, shadowed by rolling hills to the house's rere.
'The MOST friendly welcome, the MOST impressive breakfast you will ever come across. A warren of comfortable rooms, and the most wonderful care. Probably the best B&B we have ever stayed in. Violet O'Connell is one of the nicest people you will ever meet and we loved every minute staying in this smashing house.' Mr Barrett's reaction to Fortview is typical, and this is a house that renders the traditional Bridgestone editor's reserve utterly redundant: everyone from the *Bridgestone Guides*, and everyone else, just falls in love with this house. Stay for a single night, and so will you. None of us can resist archetypes.

● **OPEN:** 1 Apr-1 Oct
● **ROOMS:** Three rooms, all en suite
● **PRICE:** B&B €50 per person sharing

● **NOTES:** No credit cards accepted. Dinner strictly by prior arrangement only, €35. Two self-catering houses available. No wheelchair access. Enclosed car park. Children over 6yrs welcome in house (all ages self-catering).

● **DIRECTIONS:**
Signposted 2km from Toormore on the main Durrus road (R591). 12km from Durrus, 9km from Goleen. GPS 51.539889 -9.640589

GARNISH HOUSE

Con & Hansi Lucey
Western Road, Cork City
County Cork
☎ **+353 (0) 21-427 5111**
🖰 **www.garnish.ie**
✉ **info@garnish.ie**

'It is the best place in the world.'
That's common remark regarding
Hansi Lucey's Cork city B&B. It's
worth every word of praise.

Consider this: we were chatting to Hansi Lucey in
Garnish House one bright summer's morning in late
summer 2011 – we remember it particularly well simply
because there were so few mornings that were bright
and sunny in summer 2011 – when Hansi suddenly said,
in that disarming, sing-song Cork accent: 'You know, but
we are having our best ever year in business.' She wasn't
boasting. She was simply pointing out the vagaries of the
business, that in a year when the sun didn't shine and
when everyone is either broke or going broke, Garnish
House could still be jammers.

We put her right straight away: if Garnish was having its
best-ever year, it was because Hansi Lucey never stops
trying to get better, and every one of her team is right
there with her, trying to be their best also. It makes for
one of the great Cork destinations, a place of consummate care and hospitality, a place where the breakfasts
are benchmark – sorry, the breakfasts are the stuff of
legend – a place where they look after you.

● **OPEN:** All year
● **ROOMS:** 30 rooms, including four apartments
● **PRICE:** B&B €38-€52 per person sharing,
€59-€80 single, €129 family room

● **NOTES:** All major cards accepted. No dinner. Limited wheelchair access. Enclosed car parking. Children
welcome.
Self-catering accommodation available.

● **DIRECTIONS:**
Five minutes' walk from the city centre, opposite UCC.
GPS 51.8957 -8.4886

THE GLEN

Diana & Guy Scott
Kilbrittain
West Cork
☎ +353 (0) 23-49862
🖰 www.glencountryhouse.ie
✉ info@glencountryhouse.com

The Glen is a beautiful mid-nineteenth century country house in the most gorgeous West Cork location. And that's just the start of what makes it special.

What makes The Glen, Diana and Guy Scott's manor house close to the coast at Kilbrittain, so special? It's not simply the beauty of the house, although it is very beautiful, or its impressive vintage: it dates from 1860, and is appropriately creeper-clad. It's not even Diana's capacious skills as hostess, at which she is the best. No, there is something else going on here, in this beautiful house, which unfolds itself at the end of a long avenue of mature trees, just a stone's throw from the sea. The Glen is one of those places that seem to tap into our need and desire for nostalgia, so there is something fundamentally primal about it. You might have been reared in an elegant Gorbals tenement, but when you step in the door of The Glen you will feel you not only belong here, you will feel you were somehow born here. It's the nostalgia we feel for an imagined, privileged childhood, no matter that a bracing Gorbals childhood is the reality. And that is why The Glen is so special: the inner child is released in this special house.

● **OPEN:** April-Oct
● **ROOMS:** Four rooms and one family unit
● **PRICE:** B&B €60 per person sharing, one night, €55 two nights, €45 three nights.

● **NOTES:** Visa, Mastercard, Laser. No dinner. No wheelchair access. Secure car parking. Family unit is for two adults and two children under 16yrs. Pet friendly.

● **DIRECTIONS:**
Signposted from the R6099 approximately half way between Clonakilty and Kinsale.
GPS 51.533933 -8.700794

GORT NA NAIN FARM VEGETARIAN GUESTHOUSE

Lucy Stewart & Ultan Walsh
Ballyherkin, Nohoval, County Cork
📞 **+353 (0) 21-477 0647**
🖰 **www.gortnanain.com**
✉ **lucy@gortnanain.com**

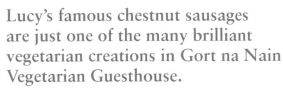

Lucy's famous chestnut sausages are just one of the many brilliant vegetarian creations in Gort na Nain Vegetarian Guesthouse.

There they are, on page 18 of Denis Cotter's great cookery book, *For the Love of Food*: 'Lucy's breakfast sausages with spiced tomato chutney'. And don't they look delicious! Who else makes chestnut sausages this good? No one. Just Lucy Stewart. That's the thing about Gort na Nain: everything looks simple, but everything is sheer class. The comfort of the farmhouse, the cheer of the hosts, the sublime nature of the food, with virtually all of it coming straight from Ultan's acclaimed organic farm. It's their own honey, their own eggs, their own chutneys, breads, pastas, the whole nine yards. So, get your feet under the table with your fellow guests to enjoy baby aubergines stuffed with courgettes and toasted pine nuts; Puy lentil and garlic potatoes wrapped up in chard parcels; home-made rhubarb ripple ice cream. You waft up the stairs to bed, and next morning, there they are: Lucy's chestnut sausages, with a poached egg straight from the hens. Ah, the good life was never better than here.

● **OPEN:** All year
● **ROOMS:** Three rooms, all en suite
● **PRICE:** €85 for two people sharing, €60 single

● **NOTES:** Vegetarian dinner, for guests only, three courses €30. Bring your own wine. Picnic baskets.
Pet friendly (booking essential)
Loc8 Code WBJ-13-SY9

● **DIRECTIONS:**
Take the airport road out of Cork. Turn left at Belgooly. Gort na Nain is five minutes further on up this road.

GOUGANE BARRA HOTEL

Neil & Katy Lucey
Gougane Barra, Macroom
County Cork
☎ **+353 (0) 26-47069**
🖱 **www.gouganebarrahotel.com**
✉ **gouganebarrahotel@eircom.net**

The GBH is the gentlest, most elemental of Irish hotels, set in a most beautiful part of beautiful West Cork.

Neil and Katy's Gougane Barra Hotel is one of the nicest hotels in Ireland. If you thought that this sort of hotel, where she cooks in the kitchen and where he meets and greets the guests, had vanished under the tsunami of zombie hotels that litter the country, then a trip to the lake of Gougane Barra will restore your soul, your sanity, and your faith in true Irish hospitality.

Mrs Lucey's food is pure lovely, a timeless, fashion-free style of unpretentious cooking that fills your heart with joy as it fills your belly with goodness. Mr Lucey is an hotelier of the old school – polite, charming, modest, attentive to every need. We love the simplicity of the rooms, we love walking in the woods, and by the beautiful, peaceful lake and the church, and we love especially the Theatre by the Lake in summertime, when a evening of d 'n' d 'n' d – dinner and drama and duvet – is one of the best experiences you can enjoy in Ireland. Gougane Barra is priceless, just priceless, the expression of Irish hospitality at its simple, quiet best.

- ● **OPEN:** early Apr-late Oct
- ● **ROOMS:** 26 rooms
- ● **PRICE:** €99 B&B per room

- ● **NOTES:** All major cards accepted. Theatre by the Lake opens mid July-late Aug. No wheelchair access. Restaurant opens breakfast & dinner from 6pm. Special rate for two nights plus one dinner. Sunday lunch.

- ● **DIRECTIONS:**
Take the R584 between Macroom & Bantry, then the L4643, following signs for Gougane Barra after the Pass. GPS 51°50' 20" N 09°19' 09" W. Locator Derreennacusha

GROVE HOUSE

Katarina Runske
Colla Road, Schull
West Cork
☎ +353 (0) 28-28067
🖱 www.grovehouseschull.com
✉ info@grovehouseschull.com

With young Nico firing out homely and delicious food in the Grove House kitchens, a third generation of the Runske family steps into the limelight.

'Stayed in Grove House in Schull, which I absolutely love!', writes Eamon Barrett. That's a typical reaction to this lovely Colla Road address. Katarina Runske is a human dynamo, one of those extraordinary people whose elemental energy is astounding to an outsider. How she does all she does we simply do not know, but she runs the house, the restaurant, the gallery and all else as if it is just an average day's work. Which, to Ms Runske, is just what it is. With her smart young son, Nico, handling things in the kitchen, Ms Runske has moved Grove House centre stage in the hospitality culture of Schull, and Nico is seemingly cut from the same cloth as his Mum: born into the business, he makes it all seem easy, and he is learning at lightning speed, so the cooking gets better and better. It's a cliché to say that Grove somehow summarises the classy bohemianism of Schull but, to tell the truth, Grove somehow summarises the classy bohemianism of Schull. It's patrician, eccentric, 100% West Cork.

- **OPEN:** all year
- **ROOMS:** Five double rooms
- **PRICE:** B&B €40 per person sharing. Single supplement €25

- **NOTES:** Visa, Laser, Mastercard, Amex. Restaurant open daily in summer, weekends only off season. Dinner always available for guests, from €22.50. Private parking. No wheelchair access.

- **DIRECTIONS:**
Take left opposite AIB, turn onto Colla Road, Grove House is about 500 metres on the right-hand side.

KILCOLMAN RECTORY

Sarah Gornall
Enniskeane
County Cork

📱 **+353 (0) 23-882 2913**
🖱 **www.kilcolmanrectory.com**
📧 **sarahjgornall@eircom.net**

Sarah Gornall is chef, gardener and
designer, and achieves all three with
a sprezzatura nonchalance in one of
West Cork's most beautiful houses.

Sarah Gornall has trained as a chef, as a gardener, and as
an interior designer, and it's as if all of her education in
all of these disciplines has been designed to lead her to
create this impeccable house, one of the smartest arriv-
als on the Irish hospitality scene in recent years. She is
one of those rare people who really can create feng shui
by putting the right object in the right place in order to
create the right aesthetic: Kilcolman has jumped straight
from *The World of Interiors*. 'Sarah Gornall is someone
who not only espouses perfection, but somehow makes
perfection look easy.' That's how *The Irish Examiner's*
Mary Leland summed up Sarah Gornall's modus oper-
andi in this beautiful 19th-century rectory. There is a
word – a superb Italian word coined by Baldassare Cas-
tiglione in his *The Book of the Courtier* in 1528 – for what
Ms Gornall achieves and the way in which she achieves
it: sprezzatura: the nonchalance that conceals effort. The
effort underscoring every detail in Kilcolman Rectory is
huge. You'd never guess.

● **OPEN:** all year
● **ROOMS:** One double/twin en suite, and three dou-
ble/twins sharing two adjacent shower rooms.
● **PRICE:** B&B €75 per person, sharing. Single €80

● **NOTES:** No credit cards. Dinner €45, advance
booking essential.

● **DIRECTIONS:** From Bandon take the Clonakilty
road. Turn right after Hosfords Garden Centre. Follow
road straight through a crossroads. Carry on until you
come to Y junction. Take left fork, and the entrance is
third on the right. GPS 51.73128 -8.86649

KNOCKEVEN HOUSE

John & Pam Mulhaire
Rushbrooke, Cobh
County Cork

📞 **+353 (0) 21-481 1778**
🖰 **www.knockevenhouse.com**
✉ **info@knockevenhouse.com**

John and Pam are masters of the great tradition of Irish hospitality, and practice it in Knockeven House.

'The finest traditions of country house hospitality.' That's what John and Pam Mulhaire promise that you will experience and enjoy in their gorgeous 1840 manor house, just outside Cobh. The interesting thing about their evocation of the tradition of hospitality, however, is the fact that Pam and John are, relatively speaking, new-comers at the game, having only opened their house to guests in 2005. But, however they acquired their mastery of the tradition, masters of it the Mulhaires most certainly are. This is a superb destination, distinguished by fastidious housekeeping, characterised by the vivacity of Pam's personality, and galvanised by her stunningly delicious breakfasts – the scrambled eggs that Pam prepares are amongst the very best in Ireland, and her buffet table is a feast for the eyes, the senses and the appetite. Wrap all these elements together in this special house, and you have a place you want to wrap yourself in, savouring every moment of the tradition of great Irish hospitality.

- **OPEN:** all year, except Christmas
- **ROOMS:** Four double rooms
- **PRICE:** B&B €50-€60 per person sharing. Single €60-€75

- **NOTES:** Visa, Mastercard, Laser accepted. No wheelchair access. Loc8 W8P -49-MD8

- **DIRECTIONS:**
Leave the N25, turn onto the R624, direction Cobh. Pass Fota, cross over bridge, take first right. At Great Gas Motors turn left and it's the first avenue on the left. GPS 51.848889 -8.318242

LANCASTER LODGE

Robert White
Lancaster Quay, Western Road,
Cork, County Cork
 +353 (0) 21-425 1125
 www.lancasterlodge.com
 info@lancasterlodge.com

Lancaster Lodge has a nifty, preppy, studenty, ambience and they do everything pro-fessionally and correctly.

Something new

People are very comfortable in Lancaster Lodge, one of those simple, comfortable lodges where you quickly find yourself feeling at home, thanks to amiable, relaxed staff and a very good level of cooking at breakfast. It may sound strange, but when John McKenna stayed here, it kind of reminded him of some campus accommodation, though there are no Jim Fitzpatrick 'Che' posters, just some hi-def American photographic landscapes in groovy colours, and MOMA prints. What was campus-like about Lancaster Lodge was the laid-back feeling, because certainly the cooking has no comparison to college food. The breakfasts are correct and good – good pancakes with bacon and maple syrup; creamed scrambled egg with smoked salmon; a choice of omelettes; and the Full Irish. It's breakfast's Greatest Hits, and it's all very nicely done, much better done than one might expect at the keen prices Lancaster charges. The location is ace, service is good, the place gleams with good housekeeping, and it's a good call.

- **OPEN:** all year
- **ROOMS:** 48 rooms, all en suite
- **PRICE:** B&B €39.50-€69 per person sharing. €86-€119 single

- **NOTES:** All major cards accepted. Full wheelchair access. 50 parking spaces. WiFi.

- **DIRECTIONS:**
At the bridge, which spans the river on Lancaster Quay, opposite Cafe Paradiso. GPS 51° 53'47"N 8°28'57" W.

LISS ARD ESTATE

Arthur Little
Russagh, Skibbereen
County Cork
📞 **+353 (0) 28-40 000**
🖱 **www.lissardestate.com**
📧 **arthur@lissardestate.com**

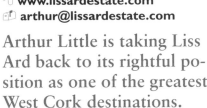

Arthur Little is taking Liss Ard back to its rightful position as one of the greatest West Cork destinations.

Something new

Friends of ours stayed at Liss Ard for several days during summer 2011 with their two kids. It is no exaggeration – truly, honestly – to say that they did not want to leave. For the kids, the house was an enchanted palace: out-of-scale, secretive, grand, Lewis Carroll meets Tim Burton by way of Enid Blyton. For the parents, the house was the West Cork country idyll writ large, a place of stunning beauty, both in the elegant, high tone house itself and in the magical gardens. Arthur Little understands and appreciates the magical space and place he runs here in Liss Ard, and he manages it with just the right tone – he is there when you need him, and he melts away when you just want to disappear into the magic of the house. Liss Ard is one of the great West Cork houses, and one of the great West Cork destinations, and Mr Little is restoring its majesty quietly and correctly. It is no exaggeration – truly, honestly – to say that when you leave Liss Ard, you leave a little piece of you behind. Better go back and get it, then.

● **OPEN:** all year, off season by arrangement.
● **ROOMS:** 15 rooms in the Country House, 10 rooms in the Lake Lodge
● **PRICE:** B&B from €65 per person

● **NOTES:** Visa, Laser, Mastercard accepted.
Wheelchair access.
Dinner from 6.30pm, table d'hôte €40

● **DIRECTIONS:**
Take the Castletownsend Road out of Skibbereen and the Estate is on your right a couple of miles out of town.
GPS 51.53 Lat, -9.25 Long

MODERN ADDRESSES

1

7 CROSS STREET
COUNTY GALWAY

2

HOTEL EUROPE
COUNTY KERRY

3

INIS MEÁIN SUITES
COUNTY GALWAY

4

THE INN @ BALLILOGUE CLOCHÁN
COUNTY KILKENNY

5

LISS ARD LAKE LODGE
COUNTY CORK

6

MOORFIELD LODGE
COUNTY DONEGAL

7

QC'S
COUNTY KERRY

8

THE ROSS
COUNTY KERRY

9

STEP HOUSE HOTEL
COUNTY CARLOW

10

NUMBER 31
COUNTY DUBLIN

LONGUEVILLE HOUSE

The O'Callaghan family
Mallow
North Cork
☎ **+353 (0) 22-47156**
🖰 **www.longuevillehouse.ie**
✉ **info@longuevillehouse.ie**

Longueville House is one of County Cork's great destinations, a self-sufficient paradise of calmness, cutting-edge cooking and hospitality.

On one of his reports to Bridgestone Central, Eamon Barrett was musing about the almost-mythical sense of relaxation that certain Irish country houses can create for their guests, that sense of super-Zen where you can completely tune-out from the cares of the world. For Mr Barrett, four houses were the leaders in the field of conjuring that sense of supreme chill-out: Gregan's Castle, Ballyvolane House, Richmond House, and Longueville House. No surprise to find Longueville up there, for this great big carnival of a country house is peaceful, serene, calm and self-absorbed. The paradox of this calm, of course, is the fact that William and Aisling O'Callaghan are the most driven, devoted and determined hosts you can find. They work hard, so you don't have to, and the fruits of their labours are astonishing, for no other country house is as self-sufficient as Longueville, where everything Mr O'Callaghan cooks is from the estate itself. The cooking is as cutting-edge as ever; the hospitality is quiet, real and genuine.

- **OPEN:** all year, weekends only Jan-Mar
- **ROOMS:** 20 rooms, all en suite
- **PRICE:** B&B €140-€180 in double room, €195-€260 in junior suite.

- **NOTES:** All major cards accepted. Dinner from 6.30pm, €29-€95. Recommended for vegetarians. Children welcome. No wheelchair facilities in rooms. Hotel will always open for groups of 20+ on half-board terms.

- **DIRECTIONS:**
5km from Mallow, travelling in direction of Killarney.
GPS 52.133515 -8.720934

NEWTOWN HOUSE

Georgie & Michael Penruddock
Kinsalebeg, Youghal
County Cork
- +353 (0) 24-94304
- www.stayatnewtown.com
- info@stayatnewtown.com

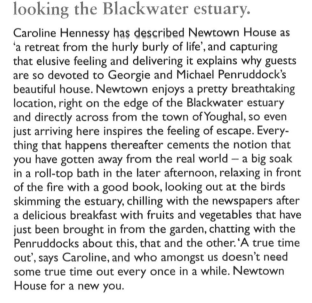

'A retreat from the hurly burly' says Caroline Hennessy of Georgie and Michael's beautiful townhouse overlooking the Blackwater estuary.

Caroline Hennessy has described Newtown House as 'a retreat from the hurly burly of life', and capturing that elusive feeling and delivering it explains why guests are so devoted to Georgie and Michael Penruddock's beautiful house. Newtown enjoys a pretty breathtaking location, right on the edge of the Blackwater estuary and directly across from the town of Youghal, so even just arriving here inspires the feeling of escape. Everything that happens thereafter cements the notion that you have gotten away from the real world – a big soak in a roll-top bath in the later afternoon, relaxing in front of the fire with a good book, looking out at the birds skimming the estuary, chilling with the newspapers after a delicious breakfast with fruits and vegetables that have just been brought in from the garden, chatting with the Penruddocks about this, that and the other. 'A true time out', says Caroline, and who amongst us doesn't need some true time out every once in a while. Newtown House for a new you.

- ● **OPEN:** All year
- ● **ROOMS:** Two rooms, both en suite
- ● **PRICE:** B&B €65 per person sharing, €100 single occupancy

- ● **NOTES:** No credit cards.
Limited wheelchair access. Picnics and light suppers by arrangement.

- ● **DIRECTIONS:**
From the village of Piltown, turn right to Ferrypoint. Proceed 0.7miles and the entrance is on the right.
GPS 51.9584 -7.8231

PIER HOUSE

Ann & Pat Hegarty
Pier Road
Kinsale, West Cork
☎ +353 (0) 21-477 4475
🖰 www.pierhousekinsale.com
✉ pierhouseaccom@eircom.net

Whether you decide that Pier House is a boutique hotel or a B&B is beside the point. What counts here above all is Ann and Pat's great hospitality.

Is the Pier House a B&B, or a small boutique hotel? You will find it described as both, and certainly it's a very stylish place if you think in terms of standard B&B design and aesthetics: the Pier is bright, colourful and vivid. Then again, it does have those features you might associate with boutique hotels, such as balconies for several of the rooms, and a fine secretive garden, with ice machines for that early evening highball before you head out to town for dinner.

But, truth be told, whatever you choose to call it, what you will remember most about Pier House is not the colourful design, or the luxury specification. What will linger in your memory will be the hospitality of Ann and Pat. Their energy drives this house, their welcome is its secret and its soul, and it sets the house apart from so many other Kinsale addresses. Mrs Hegarty makes sure everyone is looked after, she cooks lovely breakfasts and maintains a pristine house, and she does it all with charm and relish. The location is fantastic.

● **OPEN:** All year, except Christmas
● **ROOMS:** Nine rooms, all en suite
● **PRICE:** €100-€140 per room, including breakfast. Single €80

● **NOTES:**
Visa, Mastercard, Laser. No wheelchair access. No dinner. One secure parking space, otherwise public car park right next door.

● **DIRECTIONS:**
Coming from Cork, take first left at SuperValu, left at the tourist office, 50m down on right-hand side.

ROLF'S COUNTRY HOUSE

Johannes & Frederike Haffner
Baltimore Hill
Baltimore, West Cork

☎ **+353 (0) 28-20289**
🖱 **www.rolfscountryhouse.eu**
📩 **info@rolfscountryhouse.eu**

Rolf's is one of the real West Cork sports of nature, one of those special family institutions that exceed all your expectations, and then some...

Rolf's has come a long way from its early days when it operated primarily as a hostel, and today the accommodation, whilst still simple, is simply lovely: comfortable, cloistered, calm, a beautiful place in which to find yourself at any time of the year. Happily, the rooms are just as much fun as the cooking in their cosy restaurant, where the true strength is to be found in the Mittel-European specialities that Johannes really savours, such as their stroganoff, for instance, which is as good as you will get anywhere in Europe.

But aside from the comfort, the charm and the spot-on cooking, it is the energy and humour of Johannes and Frederike – and they are witty, droll, animated people – that animates Rolf's and gives it both character and soulfulness, making it a place loved by travellers and, crucially, beloved by locals: Rolf's isn't just for tourists, the locals eat here. It really is a smashing place, whether you are down in Baltimore for the boating, or just wending your way pleasurably through the wonders of West Cork.

● **OPEN:** All year, except Christmas
● **ROOMS:** 14 rooms, all en suite
● **PRICE:** €40-€50 per person sharing, including continental breakfast.

● **NOTES:** Visa, Mastercard, Laser. No wheelchair access. Holiday cottages also available. Restaurant open 12.30pm-2.30pm, 6pm-9pm (9.30pm in summer)

● **DIRECTIONS:**
On the way to Baltimore just before village turn sharp left and follow signs, approx 200m up the hill.
GPS 51.480556 -9.367779

SEA VIEW HOUSE HOTEL

Kathleen O'Sullivan
Ballylickey
Bantry, West Cork
📞 **+353 (0) 27-50462**
🖰 **www.seaviewhousehotel.com**
✉ **info@seaviewhousehotel.com**

One of the classic hotels of Ireland, Kathleen O'Sullivan's Sea View House is calm, correct and eternally enjoyable, a paragon of Irish hospitality.

Hospitality is a conundrum. It has to be unchanging, yet it has to adapt and develop. It has to be personal, and yet it must match the highest international standards. It is best if it is parochial, yet it can't be introverted. Kathleen O'Sullivan solves all these dilemmas in Sea View House Hotel, a classic Victorian manor house, which has been the home to great Irish hospitality for decades. The way Ms O'Sullivan runs her hotel is the old school way, with correct cooking, the correct service, simple and correct design, eager and correct housekeeping. The pleasures to be derived from her didactic approach to running an hotel are myriad. This may be the old school way, but that means it is the good school way, and this sense of correctness explains why so many customers regard Sea View House as one of their favourite places to stay in Ireland. Your heart leaps with anticipation and delight every time you turn up the driveway and see this elegant house once again, one of the great bastions of unchanging Irish hospitality.

- **OPEN:** mid Mar-mid Nov
- **ROOMS:** 25 rooms
- **PRICE:** B&B €120-€165 per room

- **NOTES:** All major cards accepted. Dinner in restaurant 6.45pm, Sun lunch (from Easter Sun) and lounge food daily. Dinner €35-€45. Wheelchair access. Secure parking. Pet friendly.

- **DIRECTIONS:**
On the N71 from Cork, 5km from Bantry and 13km from Glengarriff.
GPS 51.704722 -9.437222

WEST CORK HOTEL

Neil Grant
Ilen Street, Skibbereen
County Cork
📱 **+353 (0) 28-21277**
🖥 **www.westcorkhotel.com**
📧 **info@westcorkhotel.com**

Why is the West Cork Hotel so good? Because it's a very West Cork sort of hotel, if you know what we mean.

Something new

Two blokes leading from the front, and inspiring the rest of their crew. That's the story of what is happening in The West Cork Hotel, as owner Tim Looney and manager Neil Grant pull this iconic address forward. It's hard to know which of these two guys works the hardest, but the net effect of their work has been to restore the status of this much-loved hotel: once again, the WCH is a key destination, and a key part of West Cork. Everything syncs here – the cooking from chef Deane Diplock is smart and has gotten better and better as his network of local suppliers has grown. It's a great place to stay, with comfy rooms, charming staff and a liberating lack of pretension throughout. When Sally McKenna organised the first Irish Cloud Festival, it was here that the conference was held, and here where everyone dined together. The West Cork feels like an hotel: it's where you eat, meet, drink, celebrate, debate, enjoy, relax. An hotel at the heart of the community, it's a very West Cork sort of hotel, the WCH.

- **OPEN:** all year, except from 24 Dec-28 Jan
- **ROOMS:** 34 rooms, all en suite
- **PRICE:** B&B €79-€129 per room, €169 per suite

- **NOTES:** All major cards accepted.
Carvery lunch and à la carte dinner in Kennedy's Restaurant. Bar food available all day 12.30pm-9.30pm (closes 9pm off season).
Full wheelchair access.

- **DIRECTIONS:**
At the riverside, on the west side of Skibbereen
GPS 51.550555, -9271061

CASTLE MURRAY HOUSE HOTEL

Marguerite Howley
Dunkineely, County Donegal
📞 **+353 (0) 74-973 7022**
🖱 **www.castlemurray.com**
✉ **info@castlemurray.com**

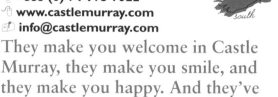

They make you welcome in Castle Murray, they make you smile, and they make you happy. And they've been doing it for more than 20 years.

Consistency, credibility, authenticity. That's what you get in Marguerite Howley's Castle Murray House, and this trio of attributes explains why Castle Murray House has been in the Bridgestone Guides ever since our first book, written way, way back in 1991. Part of Castlemurray's success is explained by the fact that Remy Dupuy has been in the kitchen since 1994, cooking house classics such as prawns and monkfish in garlic butter, tartare of Inver sea trout with blinis, or ravioli of Donegal crab. And, since 1991, we have been writing that the views from the dining room are amongst the most captivating in the entire county, and Donegal is a county that does views to beat the band. The rooms are simple and comfortable, the hospitality is genuine and fetching. 'Peopled by warm, charming staff who made us welcome, made us laugh, and made us some truly excellent food', as a correspondent noted in a fine piece of analysis which explains how Castle Murray works: they make you welcome, they make you happy.

● **OPEN:** All year, except Xmas. Weekends only Jan-Mar, Nov-Dec. Wed-Sun Apr-Jun, Sep-Oct. Open 7 days during Jul-Aug
● **ROOMS:** Ten rooms
● **PRICE:** B&B €55-€65 per person

● **NOTES:** Visa, Mastercard, Laser. Restaurant open 6.30pm-9.30pm Mon-Sat; 1.30pm-3.30pm, 6.30pm-8.30pm Sun; Dinner €45 No wheelchair access. Pet friendly.

● **DIRECTIONS:**
Castle Murray is signposted just west of Dunkineely.

LINSFORT CASTLE

Alan Rooks
Buncrana, County Donegal
📱 **+353 (0) 87 9677244**
📱 **+353 (0) 74-936 3148**
🖱 **www.linsfortcastle.com**
✉ **booking@linsfortcastle.com**

Linsfort Castle sounds grand, but Alan and Brigeen's house is the most modest, unpretentious castle you have ever stayed in. A great Donegal destination.

Alan and Brigeen's Linsfort Castle is a cult destination. 'I reckon it's possibly the best base for a holiday in Inishowen', says Caroline Byrne. 'For starters, Brigeen's gardens, while not only beautiful to walk through, produce fruit, vegetables, free-range eggs (from a clutch of Blackrock hens), and honey, all of which are served up to guests in the B&B. Inside the house, her talented eye is evident in every room, each individually and tastefully decorated, as is every nook of the house. In the old kitchen where breakfast is served every morning, an old fireplace replete with traditional hob and pots, and an old still-working wireless give a certain country elegance.' Like everyone else, Caroline fell under the spell of this charming big house and its larger-than-life hosts. Alan and Brigeen are charming, modest and generous, and they look after you and cook delicious breakfasts and they introduce you to the riches of this glorious peninsula. Believe us, but you simply will not – will not! – want to leave Linsfort!

● **OPEN:** All year
● **ROOMS:** Five rooms, three bathrooms
● **PRICE:** B&B €35 per person

● **NOTES:** No credit cards. Dinner by arrangement. Ideal for small groups or families. Comfortable lounge with library. Sun terrace. Recommended for Vegetarians. Pet friendly. No wheelchair access.

● **DIRECTIONS:**
Turn left over the bridge on northside of Buncrana. Follow Inishowen 100 and Dunree road for 4km until road forks. Take left fork. GPS 55.17171 -7.50103

McGRORY'S

Anne, John & Neil McGrory
Culdaff
County Donegal

📞 **+353 (0) 74-937 9104**
🖱 **www.mcgrorys.ie**
✉ **info@mcgrorys.ie**

Good music is often the lure for first time visitors to McGrory's, but good hospitality and good cooking will have you returning to lovely Culdaff.

The Inishowen legend that is the mighty McGrory's powers on through the years, with siblings Anne, John and Neil ladling out the hospitality as to the Donegal manner born. There is something that is so very generous about this trio as they go about their business: managing the bar, managing the restaurant and the rooms, managing the music and the gigs, so generous with their time, their energy, their knowledge and experience, that it animates the entire place. The music sessions held here are the stuff of legend, of course – Townes van Zandt live! – but McGrory's is special whether you can pick with a plectrum or pluck a pizzicato, or whether your speciality is listening to other people doing just that. Creating a destination address in such a remote, northerly place is an heroic act, but the McGrorys are wise people: they have developed slowly, organically, patiently, and they exude the culture of their area with delightful charm. This is a magical peninsula, and McGrory's your magical lodging.

● **OPEN:** All year, except Mon, Tue & Wed off season.
● **ROOMS:** 17 rooms
● **PRICE:** B&B €89-€109 per double room, €50-€69 per single room

● **NOTES:** Visa, Master, Laser, Amex. Food served in bar and restaurant Mon-Sun. Bar food served all year 12.30pm-9pm. Restaurant hours can vary according to season, so it is wise to check. Wheelchair access.

● **DIRECTIONS:**
On the main R238 between Moville and Malin Head.
GPS 55.286301 -7.165618

THE MILL

**Derek & Susan Alcorn
Figart, Dunfanaghy,
County Donegal**

📞 **+353 (0) 74-913 6985**
🖰 **www.themillrestaurant.com**
📩 **themillrestaurant@oceanfree.net**

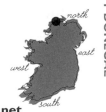

It's well worth going almost as far up north as you can go just to eat and stay at Derek and Susan's The Mill.

Derek and Susan Alcorn's The Mill made its debut in the Bridgestone Guides back in 2001, having hit the ground running with a restaurant with rooms (an r'n' r) offer that was perfectly minted, and fully formed, right from the day they opened their doors. Since then, things have simply gotten better in this most lovely house. The setting of The Mill, by the calm, mysterious New Lake on the road west out of Dunfanaghy, is serenely blissful, and the design style of the house has never needed to be altered since they opened: it felt right then and it feels right now. The hospitality from Mrs Alcorn is confident and calm, and Mr Alcorn's cooking has become simpler, more expressive and more local as time has gone by, which means what you eat here is quite simply some of the best food in the North West. Derek Alcorn is a singular cook, devoted to local foods to which he shows the ultimate respect, and he has always encouraged a great team of local talent to work alongside him. The Mill turns sweetly.

● **OPEN:** Easter to Hallowe'en, weekends off season
● **ROOMS:** Six rooms
● **PRICE:** €50 per person sharing, €75 single.

● **NOTES:** Visa, Mastercard, Laser, Amex.
No wheelchair access.
Recommended for children.

● **DIRECTIONS:**
Dunfanaghy is at the very tip of the country, coming up to Horn Head. From L'Kenny take the N56 through Dunfanaghy. The Mill is 1km past the village on right.
GPS 55.176856 -7.980311

MOORFIELD LODGE

Lin & Bobby Crossle
Letterkenny, Ramelton
County Donegal

📞 **+353 (0) 74-915 2655**
🖰 **www.moorfieldlodge.com**
📧 **lin@moorfieldlodge.com**

Moorfield Lodge is a vivid, modern house, a triumph of smart design that pulses with great spontaneous hospitality and true style.

Lin and Bobby Crossle's boutique B&B has raised the bar for levels of contemporary comfort and design in Donegal. Moorfield has three suites – The Spa; the Bayview and the Classic – and we guess that if you are in Ramelton for a special occasion then you're going to want to go the whole hog and book the Spa suite because – C.S. Lewis-style – the spa room is hidden in a wardrobe which opens out, revealing a luxurious space where you could while away half a day in pampering pleasure. Ms Crossle has hospitality in her bones, and a sincere love of good food. Her breakfast granola is superb, as is the signature strawberry and blueberry crêpe. 'We try to please the guest in every way possible. We are doing this for the love of it,' she explains. The luxury would be empty without the friendliness the couple exude, and it is this charm that animates Moorfield. The Crossles spent a long time looking for just the right property to develop as a B&B, but even if they ran a Nissen hut, you would stay with them.

● **OPEN:** All year except Christmas and Jan-Feb
● **ROOMS:** Three suites
● **PRICE:** B&B €100 for the Classic, €135 for the Bayview, €150 for the Spa Suite

● **NOTES:** No credit cards. Not suitable for children. Wheelchair access with assistance - please ask.

● **DIRECTIONS:**
From Letterkenny's Polestar roundabout head toward Ramelton. 2 miles past the Silver Tassie Hotel, pass X-sign, squiggly road sign then turn left at the next cross. GPS 55.0094833 -7.658445

WITH ROOMS

1

CASTLE MURRAY HOUSE HOTEL
COUNTY DONEGAL

2

THE COURTHOUSE
COUNTY LEITRIM

3

CULLINAN'S
COUNTY CLARE

4

THE OLD POST INN
COUNTY CAVAN

5

MacNEAN TOWNHOUSE
COUNTY CAVAN

6

THE MILL
COUNTY DONEGAL

7

MORRISSEY'S
COUNTY CLARE

8

QC'S
COUNTY KERRY

9

THE TANNERY
COUNTY WATERFORD

10

WILD HONEY INN
COUNTY CLARE

RATHMULLAN HOUSE

The Wheeler family
Lough Swilly, Rathmullan
County Donegal
📞 **+353 (0) 74-915 8188**
🖰 **www.rathmullanhouse.com**
📧 **info@rathmullanhouse.com**

Rathmullan House offers one of the most authentic Irish country house experiences, thanks to a total lack of pretension. Few airs, many graces.

'Most beguiling of all, there was also an indefinable comfy-ness about the hotel; grand, but lived-in, few airs, but many graces'.

That's Judith Woods, writing in *The Daily Telegraph* about Rathmullan House, and you couldn't sum up the place better than Mrs Woods' fine aphorism: few airs, but many graces. That's Rathmullan alright, a place where the Wheeler family show their dynamic hospitality, their generosity, and their genius for setting the mood at just the right pitch. You need a few days to get into Rathmullan, to slow down to its pace, to get at the level of those many graces. It's a most beloved house, especially for regular visitors from Northern Ireland who adore it. But the calmness is created simply because the Wheelers work so hard, and there is a continual smorgasbord of events and happenings to divert and delight everyone. Kelan McMicheal's food is at just the right pitch also, ennobling superb local foods with sympathetic culinary skills. Few airs, many graces.

● **OPEN:** Open all year, apart from mid Jan-mid Feb and closed mid week Nov & Dec
● **ROOMS:** 34 rooms
● **PRICE:** €85-€140 per person

● **NOTES:** Visa, Laser, Mastercard, Amex. Wheelchair access. Swimming pool. Pet friendly. Family rooms. Loc8 code BNJ-09-X76

● **DIRECTIONS:**
In Rathmullan, turn left at the Mace shop. Go north through the village, past the Blue Church, turn right at black gates. GPS 55.09871 -7.53443

ABERDEEN LODGE

Pat Halpin
53-55 Park Avenue, Ballsbridge
Dublin 4
📞 **+353 (0) 1-283 8155**
🖱 **www.halpinsprivatehotels.com**
📧 **reservations@halpinsprivatehotels.com**

Pat and Anne's Aberdeen
Lodge is the quintessential
Ballsbridge townhouse: calm,
gracious, sophisticated, chic.

Every time the McKennas have stayed in Aberdeen
Lodge, Pat and Anne Halpin's high and handsome
Victorian red brick on leafy Park Avenue in handsome
Ballsbridge, we have had nothing but a great time. It's the
sort of destination that our kids, who have known Aberdeen Lodge ever since they were bairns, love returning
to, and it's especially delightful to have such a memora-
ble place to stay in your catalogue of happy childhood
memories, a house that is a benchmark for hospitality,
for comfort, for great cooking, for chilling, for enjoying
whenever it is time to head north from West Cork and
visit the Big Smoke. Aberdeen works because everything
is done correctly, as it should be and as it has to be,
but there is no stuffiness or formality to Pat and Anne,
and their professionalism is cloaked in a quiet, modest
confidence. The hospitality is primal, the housekeeping is
meticulous, the cooking is simply superb, and offers one
of the best breakfasts that you will find in the capital. It's
a special place, Aberdeen Lodge. Just ask the McKennas.

● **OPEN:** All year
● **ROOMS:** 17 rooms, including two suites
● **PRICE:** €65-€90 per person sharing, €99-€120
single

● **NOTES:** All major cards accepted. Light 'drawing
room' menu, €8-€15 per course, extensive wine list.
Parking. Wheelchair access. Not suitable for children
under 7yrs. Concierge service.

● **DIRECTIONS:**
Just down from the Sydney Parade DART station.
GPS 53.325017 -6.213247

ARIEL HOUSE

Deirdre McDonald
50-54 Lansdowne Road
Dublin 4

☎ **+353 (0) 1-668 5512**
✉ **reservations@ariel-house.net**
🖰 **www.ariel-house.net**

Ariel is a great Dublin destination with brilliant food and service, superbly run by Deirdre McDonald. Breakfast is one of the best in the city.

So, that's John McKenna over there in the conservatory of the dining room at Ariel and those two bedraggled teenagers with him are his children: Connie and Sam. They may look like – they do look like – two street waifs whom McKenna has just rescued from a rubbish tip commune in Rio, but the truth is that they are just back from three days at the Leeds Festival, which is why they look like rubbish foragers. Three days of camping in the mud and you too can look like a Third World orphan. But, they are coming back to civilisation, after a comfy night's sleep, and breakfast in Ariel is surely one of the best ways to do just that: brown bread, scones, banana bread; grapefruit with honey and sugar; French toast with crème fraiche and berries; poached eggs and smoked salmon with beurre blanc; a stack of pancakes with maple syrup and grilled bacon. It's all superb: the service is friendly, the house is buzzing, and Deirdre McDonald runs a great show in Ariel. The McKenna children will go home, and sleep for a week.

- **OPEN:** All year, except Christmas
- **ROOMS:** 37 rooms, all en suite
- **PRICE:** B&B from €79 per room

- **NOTES:**
Visa, Mastercard, Laser, Amex. Facilities for wheelchair customers. Complimentary car parking.
Afternoon tea served 2pm-5pm daily.
Children welcome.

- **DIRECTIONS:**
Right beside the Aviva stadium.
GPS 53.334153 -6.231103

BROOK'S HOTEL

Anne McKiernan
Drury Street
Dublin 2

☏ **+353 (0) 1-670 4000**
🖰 **www.brookshotel.ie**
🖂 **reservations@brookshotel.ie**

*Every member of staff in
Brooks Hotel is a character,
which is why Brooks Hotel is
simply the best hotel in Dublin.*

It might seem strange to say it about an hotel, but one of the things that makes Brooks so special – that make it the best hotel in Dublin, to be frank – is that it has a Mom'n'Pop feel, thanks to manager Anne McKiernan and chef Patrick McLarnon. Their brilliance gives Brooks an entirely different feel from other city centre addresses: Brooks feels personal, intimate, and real, a place run by people, whereas other places feel they are run by a manual, and consequently feel impersonal, indifferent and unreal.

As you would expect of two quietly larger-than-life and surprising characters, the team who work with them are as vivid as the manager and the chef, fascinating characters in their own right, full of stories, full of wisdom. They all sync together perfectly, doing their work with aplomb from the brilliant breakfasts, right through lunch and dinner, and on to a late night whiskey in the bar. Brooks exemplifies the hotel-ness of an hotel, offering not just a welcome, but a real sense of wellbeing.

- **OPEN:** All year including Christmas
- **ROOMS:** 98 bedrooms, including three suites
- **PRICE:** €80-€90 standard double, per person sharing, single supplement €65

- **NOTES:** Visa, Mastercard, Amex. Restaurant open breakfast & dinner. Bar serves food 10am-6pm, & 6pm-10pm. Fitness suite. Pillow menu. Wi-Fi.

- **DIRECTIONS:**
Drury Street is parallel to Grafton St, between Grafton St and Sth Gt George's St, in the centre of Dublin. GPS 53.3421615   -6.2634513

NUMBER 31

Noel Conroy
31 Lower Leeson Street
Dublin 4

☏ **+ 353 (0) 1-676 5011**
🖥 **www.number31.ie**
📧 **info@number31.ie**

No other house is like Number 31.
Half modernist mews, half elegant
Georgian townhouse, it seems to exist
in two worlds, in two timeframes.

Noel Conroy's house has to be the strangest double act
in Dublin's hospitality history. One half ultra-modernist
mews, one half traditional Georgian townhouse, it is
utterly unique. That it works, indeed the fact that there
seems to be no tension between the two halves of the
house, is down to the attention to detail that has been
lavished on each room –The Georgians are appositely
Georgian, muted and restrained and dignified, the
modernists are unapologetically modern, colourful and
brutalist – and it helps also that the team here are just
as cool as the house itself. They produce one of the very
best breakfasts in the city – *The Daily Telegraph* once
called the Number 31 breakfasts 'the talk of the town',
which is stretching it a bit, but not too much. Best of all,
it's a house that always feels new and alive, no matter
how many times you have stayed here, no matter how
many new people you have met in the 'conversation pit'
drawing room. It's a classic design, classic house, and a
classic experience every time you stay.

● **OPEN:** all year, including Christmas
● **ROOMS:** 21 bedrooms

● **PRICE:** €140-€220 per room

● **NOTES:**
Visa, Mastercard, Laser, Amex
No wheelchair access

● **DIRECTIONS:**
At the upper end of Lower Leeson Street, near the
corner with Fitzwilliam Place, in the centre of Dublin.

PEMBROKE HOUSE

Fiona Teehan
90 Pembroke Road, Ballsbridge
Dublin 4
📞 **+353 (0) 1-660 0277**
🖱 **www.pembroketownhouse.ie**
📧 **info@pembroketownhouse.ie**

Pembroke House is a real feel-good destination, and Fiona Teehan's team is the hardest working crew in the city, hopelessly devoted to their guests.

A beautiful location on tree-lined Pembroke Road is just one of the major assets of Fiona Teehan's Pembroke House. More importantly, the exceptionally fine staff manage to trump the fine location, and in doing so they bring alive the grandeur of this lovely Georgian house. Inside, the bedrooms are calming and very, very comfortable, stylish without being enslaved to design, so their focus is on a comfort that makes you feel very good indeed, especially when the staff arrive with some tea and hand-made biscuits to calm the weary traveller. That feel-good factor is an key element of Pembroke House, because it's one of those elements that is hard to capture, hard to conjure, hard to create. But when someone gets it – as Ms Teehan and her team do – then it means that the guest is a very happy person indeed. They have worked assiduously over the last year and more to make their breakfasts something special, giving the house another attraction, and the staff look after you properly, in that waggish Dublin way which is so fine.

- **OPEN:** All year, except four weeks at Christmas
- **ROOMS:** 48 rooms, all en suite (incl seven suites)
- **PRICE:** from €99 per room

- **NOTES:** All major cards accepted. Parking complimentary for residents. Car park entrance is on Baggot Lane. Wheelchair access.

- **DIRECTIONS:**
Pembroke Road is at the Southern end of Upper Baggot Street. Pembroke Townhouse faces Raglan Road with large lanterns on each side of the front door.
GPS 53.332476 -6.23806

ANGLER'S RETURN

Lynn Hill
Toombeola, Roundstone
Connemara, County Galway
📞 **+ 353 (0) 95-31091**
🖱 **www.anglersreturn.com**
✉ **info@anglersreturn.com**

Make sure to stay at least three nights at Lynn Hill's beautiful Roundstone cottage, an aesthetic Connemara treasure, always picture postcard perfect.

Lynn Hill's Angler's Return is a little bit like Kelly's Hotel, of Rosslare. 'To really enjoy the "real" feel of this house,' Lynn says, 'and to truly relax, one needs three days' stay here, in order to unwind. So many guests suggested this to me last summer, and the ones who stayed a week or more were the happiest, believe it or not!' We can believe it. Angler's Return, like Kelly's Hotel, is a house that you need to lower yourself into, as if it were a beautiful, big, bubble bath. Just staying one night and rushing through Connemara, is madness personified. You have to let this place into your soul. And when you do that, when you get Zen, you suddenly see the birds, and hear the bees – especially if you are lying on a rug in the pretty garden of the Angler's Return! And then there is a cracking fire in the evening time in the sitting room, looking out at the lakes and the sunset and maybe a simple, delicious dinner cooked by Lynn. Now, isn't that the real Connemara!? You will surely never be the same again.

● **OPEN:** open Feb-Nov
● **ROOMS:** five rooms, one en suite, four other rooms share two adjacent bathrooms

● **PRICE:** from €90 per double room

● **NOTES:**
No credit cards.
Not suitable for children under 8 years, babes in arms welcome.

● **DIRECTIONS:**
Four miles, on the Galway side, of Roundstone.

BALLYNAHINCH CASTLE

Patrick O'Flaherty
Ballinafad, Recess, Connemara
County Galway
📞 **+353 (0) 95-31006**
🖱 **www.ballynahinch-castle.com**
📖 **bhinch@iol.ie**

Ballynahinch Castle is a star destination where hospitality, service and cooking synthesise in calm perfection.

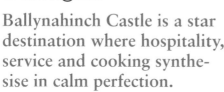

So here is what Sam, PJ and John McKenna had for dinner on their last trip to Ballynahinch: slow-cooked McGeough's pork neck in air-dried ham; galantine of duck foie gras and confit duck leg; tomato and ginger soup; raspberry sorbet; assiette of McGeough's Irish pork; McGeough's beef filet; black sole cooked on the bone; pecan pie and vanilla ice cream. It was all delicious, proof of Xin Sun's excellence as a cook, and his smartness in sourcing his meats from James McGeough of Oughterard. Breakfast-time, meanwhile, offered a superb buffet table and beautifully cooked food, and the dining room is always a special place in which to enjoy such peachy cooking. Good judgement and excellent staff are the keys to Ballynahinch, as well as a jaw-dropping estate which is essentially a world-unto-itself. The river wends through the estate, and whilst you can't step into the same river twice, you can step into the same Ballynahinch Castle twice, for it is constant, unchanging, faithfully excellent: a Connemara classic.

● **OPEN:** All year, except Feb and Christmas
● **ROOMS:** 40 rooms, including three suites
● **PRICE:** €80-€245 per person sharing, single supplement €40

● **NOTES:** All major cards accepted. Dinner in restaurant, €60. No wheelchair access. Private fishery, walking routes and hikes.

● **DIRECTIONS:**
From Galway, take signs for Clifden (N59). At Recess you will begin to see their signs.
GPS 53.4602166 -9.86311666

CONNEMARA COAST HOTEL

Ann Downey (General Manager)
Furbo, Galway
County Galway

📞 + 353 (0) 91-592108
🖱 www.connemaracoast.ie
✉ info@connemaracoast.ie

Hotelier Charles Synnott runs hotels on both the east and west coasts, and runs both of them superbly well, epitomising the art of hotel-keeping.

Charles Synnott understands that to run an hotel, you need to be an hotelier, that most noble, and difficult, of vocations. In fact, Mr Synnott runs two hotels in this book, and it is their difference, and their distinctiveness, that appeals to us. Brooks Hotel in Dublin is the only Dublin hotel in this book, and it is the quintessential city hotel. But the Connemara Coast, then, is a quintessential resort hotel, a place to escape to from the city, a place to enjoy sea air, good food, a beautiful art collection, along with excellent service from a crack team who know their work inside out, led by manager Ann Downey. The Coast is a place to relax, and the staff manage to create the Ocean Liner Effect perfectly: when you stay here, you are away from it all, the workaday world has departed, and you and your family are on vacation. That's the Ocean Liner Effect. To create and maintain this feeling is the true art and craft of the hotelier, and you will rarely see it practised better than it is practised in this special West Coast getaway.

● **OPEN:** open all year except Christmas
● **ROOMS:** 141 rooms, standard, superior & executive
● **PRICE:** €89-€125 per person sharing. Supplements (around €50) apply to superior rooms and suites.

● **NOTES:** Visa, Mastercard, Laser, Amex. Mid-week offers available. Wheelchair access. Two restaurants, cocktail bar and pub.

● **DIRECTIONS:**
From Galway, follow signs for Clifden and Oughterard. The Connemara Coast is on this road on the left, in the village of Furbo, just after Barna.

10 GREAT

TRADITIONAL ADDRESSES

1

BALLYMALOE HOUSE
COUNTY CORK

2

BALLYVOLANE HOUSE
COUNTY CORK

3

COOPERSHILL HOUSE
COUNTY SLIGO

4

DELPHI LODGE
COUNTY GALWAY

5

LINSFORT CASTLE
COUNTY DONEGAL

6

MOUNT VERNON
COUNTY CLARE

7

MOY HOUSE
COUNTY CLARE

8

RICHMOND HOUSE
COUNTY WATERFORD

9

SEA MIST HOUSE
COUNTY GALWAY

10

SHEEDY'S
COUNTY CLARE

7 CROSS STREET

Olivia O'Reilly
7 Cross Street, Galway
County Galway
📠 **+353 (0) 91-530100**
🖱 **www.7crossstreet.com**
📧 **info@7crossstreet.com**

A micro-sized hotel with chic rooms, and the location simply can't be beaten, as central as Galway gets.

Something new

Paris has lots of little hotels where you walk through a single narrow door, then down a narrow entrance to a little reception desk and, having checked in, you climb steep stairs to the warren of little bedrooms. If you are lucky, you have a view of the Parisian skyline. If you don't, you console yourself with the thought that you are still smack in the city centre. Olivia O'Reilly's No 7 Cross Street is one of those hotels – the narrow doorway on the street, the narrow hall, the tiny reception space, the tiny rooms, the city centre location, the bustle and noise, and it brought back to us floods of memories of staying in inexpensive Parisian hotels when we used to backpack. So, No 7 suits us perfectly, and if you like petite rooms – let's call them intimate – and cheek-by-jowl eating, then you will love this chic little space on Cross Street. It would be impossible to be more central in Galway city – if you don't fancy the noise, they also have a fine house on Nun's Island – but we love the at-the-heart-of-the-city feeling, that true Galway chutzpah.

● **OPEN:** open all year
● **ROOMS:** 10 rooms, all en suite
● **PRICE:** €65-€99 per person sharing.

● **NOTES:** Visa, Mastercard, Laser. Not suitable for young children. No wheelchair access due to development restrictions. Parking available 3 minutes away at reduced overnight rate. Continental self-service breakfast.

● **DIRECTIONS:**
In the very centre of Galway city, Cross Street runs from the main pedestrian walkway High Street, and the Town House is adjacent to Neachtain's Pub.

DELPHI LODGE

Peter Mantle
Leenane, Connemara
County Galway
📞 **+353 (0) 95-42222**
🖱 **www.delphilodge.ie**
📧 **res@delphilodge.ie**

It's not just the many charms of Delphi Lodge that make it unique. It's also that they know what they don't want to be.

The reason Peter Mantle's country house and estate is world-renowned is not just because of what it is, but also because of what it is not. Yes, it is an especially beautiful house in one of the most beautiful places in Ireland – if not the world. And yes it is beloved of fishermen hoping for a salmon, and it is beloved of food lovers who relish Cliodna Prendergasts's creative and ingenious cooking, whilst wine buffs can lose the run of themselves in the incredible selection of wines on the list. But these things don't explain Delphi's renown, for equally important to its capacious assets is the fact that Delphi doesn't try to be an hotel, or to ape hotel-style service. It has stubbornly and determinedly set its face against the modern blandness that people think of as luxury. So, instead it is quaint, a place that is comfortable with itself, which means you will be comfortable with it too. In Delphi, they know what they can do best, and their best is what they do. It's a simple thing, but it demands a quiet confidence.

● **OPEN:** Mar-Sep (house parties 18+ off season)
● **ROOMS:** 12 rooms, all en suite (seven with lake view)
● **PRICE:** from €99 per person. Single supplement and lakeview upgrade €33.

● **NOTES:** Visa & Mastercard. Dinner, 8pm, communal table €49. Wheelchair accessible, but not fully disabled-friendly. Flyfishing. Not suitable for young children.

● **DIRECTIONS:**
12km northwest of Leenane on the Louisburgh road. In woods on left about half mile after the Adventure Spa. GPS 53.631916 -9.747190

DEVON DELL

Berna Kelly
47 Devon Park
Lower Salthill, Galway city
📞 **+353 (0) 91-528306**
🖰 **www.devondell.com**
📧 **devondel@iol.ie**

Every morning Berna Kelly prepares breakfast as if it is a brand new, bespoke creation, being fashioned for the very first time, and just for you.

Devon Dell may be a simple house, set in a quiet cul-de-sac a short stroll from the centre of Galway, but it's precisely the kind of place that Galway does well: individual; aspirational, a bit naive, pure delight. In Berna Kelly's house, the housekeeping that you experience, the stellar standards of cooking, the thoughtfulness of the hospitality, are exactly the things that Galway citizens do the best. It's pure Galway, in the way that some places are pure West Cork. Hard to define, but you know it when you get it. And that is what you get in Devon Dell: pure Galway. Mrs Kelly has an impish, endless curiosity when it comes to cooking. Each morning, it is as if the breakfast has been fashioned with a beginner's mind, so everything seems newly minted, full of culinary possibilities, crafted with generosity and openness, and without cliché or rote. It is a marvellous performance, and it is created every morning with the fastidiousness of a true professional, and it speaks of the generous zeitgeist of Galway. The city spirit is here.

- ● **OPEN:** Mar-Oct
- ● **ROOMS:** 2 double rooms, 1 twin & 1 single, en suite
- ● **PRICE:** €45 per person sharing

- ● **NOTES:** No credit cards. No wheelchair access. No facilities for very young children. Street parking.

- ● **DIRECTIONS:**
Find Fr Griffin Rd, and follow to T-junction, where you take left into Lr Salthill Rd. After approx 500m, having passed two pubs, take first right. Go 100m to fork in road, take left and very sharp left into cul-de-sac.
GPS 53.265192 -9.073872

DOLPHIN BEACH

The Foyle family
Lower Sky Road, Clifden
Connemara, County Galway
📞 **+ 353 (0) 95-21204**
🖱 **www.dolphinbeachhouse.com**
✉ **stay@dolphinbeachhouse.com**

Our visiting editor, Elizabeth Field,
pays homage to the wonderful idyll
that is Dolphin Beach. What follows is
a tone poem to pleasure...

'Dolphin Beach embodies all I would wish to have in a
small hotel. Gorgeous views over the Atlantic Ocean,
Slyne Head and Ballyconneely Bay; sparkling clear
Western light and fresh breezes; relaxing peace and
quiet; wonderful locally sourced food and inimitable Irish
hospitality. The small details are all there: the comfort-
ing pot of tea and biscuits when you arrive; perfect
beds with crisp linen; beautiful books to leaf through
in the front room; home-made breads and jam. I love
the spare, Scandinavian-inspired modern decor: lots of
wood, lots of windows, rooms that open directly onto a
patio. Clodagh Foyle has innkeeping in her blood and it
shows. She effortlessly juggles a million household tasks
and is always ready with a smile. A brief meander up
Sky Road after a summer dinner gave us but the baaaah
of sheep, the rustling of trees, the smell of honeysuckle
and a drawn-out sunset over the water. This is the place
I would choose to truly unwind.' Ahhh, only in beautiful
Dolphin Beach.

● **OPEN:** mid Feb-mid Nov
● **ROOMS:** Nine en suite rooms
● **PRICE:** €60-€85 per person sharing. Single supple-
ment €20

● **NOTES:**
Dinner if booked in advance, €37. Visa, Mastercard, Laser.
Limited wheelchair access. Loc8 Code is KLR-90-R66

● **DIRECTIONS:**
Take the Sky road out of Clifden, take the lower fork for
1 mile. It's the house on the sea side.
GPS 53.497778 -10.094722

THE HERON'S REST

Sorcha Mulloy
16a Longwalk, Spanish Arch
Galway, County Galway
📱 **+353 (0) 86-337 9343**
🖱 **www.theheronsrest.com**
✉ **theheronsrest@gmail.com**

Sorcha Mulloy's riverside B&B has the country's most original breakfast, and a visiting heron, called Jack. Really. Trust us.

There is a heron, you know, who likes to rest right outside Sorcha Mulloy's riverside house at the Spanish Arch. He's called Jack, and we took a picture of him last time we stayed, in the afternoon just as we arrived. He's photogenic, and patient, standing still long enough so we could get the picture on our 'phone. Only in Galway. The rest of the country is littered with houses called Sea View (no view of the sea), Orchard Grove (no orchard, no grove), Chez Nous (wrong country). But, in Galway, Heron's Rest means just that: the place where the heron – Jack – comes to rest. You couldn't make it up. Mind you, you could hardly make Sorcha Mulloy up, either. There is no more meticulous hostess in Ireland. But she's funky, too, and she creates a breakfast that has no parallel in Ireland. Last time we started with beautiful fruit salad with goji berries and yogurt, then pearl barley porridge with poached cinnamon pears and honeyed dates. We felt like we could have taken to the skies, just like Jack.

● **OPEN:** 1 May-31 Oct
● **ROOMS:** Three double rooms, two singles: double rooms en suite or private bath, single sharing bathroom.
● **PRICE:** €65-€80 per person sharing

● **NOTES:**
All major credit cards accepted. No wheelchair access. Street parking in front of house. Children welcome.

● **DIRECTIONS:**
Follow signs for East Galway and Docks. Turn left at the Limerick Steamhouse and follow the road around to the right. Heron's Rest is facing the water.

INIS MEÁIN SUITES

Ruairí & Marie-Therese de Blacam
Inis Meáin, Aran Islands
County Galway

📱 **+ 353 (0) 86-826 6026**
🖱 **www.inismeain.com**
✉ **post@inismeain.com**

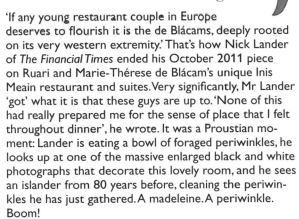

A Proustian moment, with
a periwinkle rather than a
madeleine, for the *FT*'s man on
Inis Meain. That's the feeling.

'If any young restaurant couple in Europe
deserves to flourish it is the de Blácams, deeply rooted
on its very western extremity.' That's how Nick Lander
of *The Financial Times* ended his October 2011 piece
on Ruari and Marie-Thérèse de Blácam's unique Inis
Meain restaurant and suites. Very significantly, Mr Lander
'got' what it is that these guys are up to. 'None of this
had really prepared me for the sense of place that I felt
throughout dinner', he wrote. It was a Proustian moment: Lander is eating a bowl of foraged periwinkles, he
looks up at one of the massive enlarged black and white
photographs that decorate this lovely room, and he sees
an islander from 80 years before, cleaning the periwinkles he has just gathered. A madeleine. A periwinkle.
Boom!
No other place conveys such a sense of place as Inis
Meain. It is unforgettable, because everything is so
simple, so elemental (Mr Lander also raved about the
spuds). Just make sure to book early. Nowhere like it.

● **OPEN:** April-Sept
● **ROOMS:** four large suites
● **PRICE:** B&B €250-€350 per person. Two-night stay
minimum. Packages available.

● **NOTES:** Visa, Mastercard, Laser. Restaurant open for
Dinner, main courses €16-€35.

● **DIRECTIONS:**
Take the ferry from Rossaveal, or plane from Inverin.
You find the house in the middle of the island, pass the
only pub on your right, take the next right, then look
out for stone building 100m on your left.

KILMURVEY HOUSE

Treasa & Bertie Joyce
Kilmurvey Bay, Inis Mór
Aran Islands, County Galway
☎ **+353 (0) 99-61218**
📧 **kilmurveyhouse@eircom.net**
🖰 **www.kilmurveyhouse.com**

Don't make the mistake of charging around Inis Mor and thinking you've 'done' the Aran Islands. You need to stay at Kilmurvey to get the magic.

Most visitors to the Aran Islands make a disastrous mistake: they don't stay here. Instead, they arrive on the morning ferry, scoot around the island on a bike or in a minibus – don't get us started about how reckless those minibus drivers are, or what damage they do to the island! – and then they leave on an afternoon ferry. There! Aran Islands done! Next?!

That's not how you do it. To understand these mystical islands requires one thing: it requires you to stop. For at least two days, four days are even better. So, book yourself into Treasa and Berties's lovely house. Swim in Kilmurvey Bay. Trek the island to see the stones and flowers and waves and colours. Explore Dun Aengus. Relax in the bars of Kilronan. Enjoy Treasa's stupendous breakfasts, amongst the nicest you will ever eat. Enjoy Bertie's hospitality. Borrow a bike and cycle slowly around the perimeter of Inis Mor. Now you are getting it, now you get it. Aran has to sink into your soul. Kilmurvey House is your portal for that pleasure.

- **OPEN:** 1 Apr-16 Oct
- **ROOMS:** 12 rooms, all en suite (seven family rooms)
- **PRICE:** €45-€50 per person sharing. Single €60-€65

- **NOTES:**
No wheelchair access. Dinner by arrangement only. Complimentary bus to Kilronan for dinner, or evening snack menu served in the house.

- **DIRECTIONS:**
The house is a further 7km from the ferry port. On arrival, take any one of the tour buses.

THE QUAY HOUSE

Paddy & Julia Foyle
Beach Road, Clifden
Connemara, County Galway
📞 **+353 (0) 95-21369**
🖥 **www.thequayhouse.com**
📧 **res@thequayhouse.com**

'Honestly, Irish hospitality at its best is unbeatable. That Foyle family is something else!' Something Else!

Elizabeth Field's reaction to Paddy and Julia Foyle's gorgeous house articulates every duality that makes this house extra-special: peaceful yet dynamic; stylish yet relaxed; private yet public, a world apart. 'This place has tons of style: overstuffed sofas and chairs, walls chock-a-block with paintings and ornaments; plump pillows; meandering corridors. Our room on the third floor overlooked the quay. It was HUGE, with a canopy bed, comfortable seating, and I think a fireplace. Also a lovely old-fashioned large bathroom. The breakfast was outstanding: scrambled eggs with smoked salmon; porridge with berry compote; and all the fixings of the full Irish, something I really miss on the other side of the pond. The Foyles are absolutely dynamic: funny, warm, urbane and welcoming. It's a 3-minute walk to town, which is quite nice, as the town can get pretty crowded. So you feel like you're in your own private, rambling, wisteria-covered residence. I wouldn't want to stay anyplace else in Clifden.'

● **OPEN:** mid Mar-early Nov
● **ROOMS:** 14 en suite rooms, including rooms with kitchens
● **PRICE:** B&B from €75 per person sharing, €100-€120 single rate

● **NOTES:** Visa, Mastercard, Laser. No dinner. Wheelchair access. Street parking.

● **DIRECTIONS:**
The Quay House is down on the quays, past the small playground, and overlooking the harbour.
GPS 53.463525 -10.033264

RENVYLE HOUSE

**Ronnie Counihan
Renvyle, Connemara
County Galway**
☎ **+353 (0) 95-43511**
🖰 **www.renvyle.com**
📧 **info@renvyle.com**

A coastal country house that is unlike any other address in Ireland, Renvyle marries great hospitality and food.

Ronnie and Tim, manager and chef of Renvyle House, are one of the great double acts in Irish hospitality and food. Between them, Mr Ronnie Counihan and Mr Tim O'Sullivan have created a manifesto for Renvyle that is one of the most compelling examples of contemporary Irish ingenuity. It means that Renvyle looks like an hotel and has the scale of an hotel, but feels more like a country house. It means that the food is cutting edge, and yet is also simple and unpretentious, earthy and agrestic, smartly sourced from excellent local artisan suppliers. It means that Renvyle feels traditional, yet is as modern as you need it to be. Reconciling all these seeming contradictions takes a particular form of genius, and these two genial blokes have it in spades. Genial geniuses seems just the right way to describe them, and this beautiful house is fortunate to have two guys who so completely understand it and appreciate it, and are thereby able to present it at its best to guests. There is no more soulful, relaxing place.

● **OPEN:** Mar-Nov. Open for Christmas.
● **ROOMS:** 70 rooms
● **PRICE:** B&B €40-€120 per person. No single supplement. Look out for offers on website.

● **NOTES:** All major cards accepted. Restaurant serves dinner, 7pm-9pm, €50. Outdoor heated swimming pool and golf. Full wheelchair access. Pet friendly.

● **DIRECTIONS:**
The hotel is signposted from Kylemore. At Letterfrack, turn right, and travel 6.5km to hotel gates.
GPS 53.609167 -9.999167

SEA MIST HOUSE

Sheila Griffin
Clifden, Connemara
County Galway
📱 **+353 (0) 95-21441**
🖱 **www.seamisthouse.com**
🖂 **sheila@seamisthouse.com**

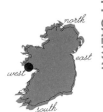

So, how do you define the essence of *Bridgestone?* What makes an address one of the 100 Best? Sheila Griffin defines the essence: she's different.

A stone-clad, handsome house dating from the 1820's, set just down the seaward road off the main square in Clifden, Sheila Griffin's Sea Mist B&B is one of those houses that define the essence of Bridgestone.
How do you do that? How do you clock up the list of details that means you earn entry into a book like this? Well, one of the signifiers we look for is people who are happy to be different. So, at Sea View, there are no televisions in the bedrooms. Sheila Griffin takes the opposite point of view from those who think every room has to have a flat screen TV along with a stereo and wi-fi and whatnot. Ms Griffin knows that if you are in Connemara, you should be out on the Twelve Bens, or at least enjoying her lovely garden, or relaxing in the aesthetic of her beautiful house. So, she does things differently, and we like that, just as we like the fact that she cooks with imagination and makes scrummy breakfasts, and graces her house with a cool bohemian ambience. The courage to be different: that's Bridgestone.

● **OPEN:** Mar-Nov
● **ROOMS:** Four rooms, all en suite
● **PRICE:** €40-€60 per person sharing, single supplement €15-€25

● **NOTES:** Visa, Mastercard, Laser, Amex. No dinner. No wheelchair access. No facilities for children. Limited enclosed parking.

● **DIRECTIONS:**
Beside the Bank of Ireland, a little away from the town centre.
Sat Nav 53.4882 -10.0244.

BROOK LANE HOTEL

Dermot & Una Brennan
Kenmare
County Kerry

☎ **+353 (0) 64-664 2077**
⌂ **www.brooklanehotel.com**
✉ **info@brooklanehotel.com**

Dermot and Una Brennan's
22-bedroom boutique hotel
is modest, meticulous and
endlessly self-improving.

Something new

Dermot and Una Brennan are like Steve Jobs: they
tweak, endlessly, endlessly, seeking to improve everything they do, whether it's in the comfy, cosy confines
of the Brook Lane, or in No 35, their hip restaurant in
the centre of Kenmare, just a couple of minutes' walk
from the hotel itself. Like Jobs, they scarcely need to
tweak, for they have a habit of getting things right from
the outset. But they are restless hoteliers, and intensely
self-critical, so they worry about the breakfast in the
hotel – it's great: don't miss their breads, and the brilliant
Sneem black pudding – and the food in Casey's Bistro
– don't miss the signature chowder and the signature
gourmet burger – and the menu in No 35 – don't miss
the incredibly funky pizzas. It's the happy customer who
benefits from all this tweaking, however, and the Brook
Lane is one of those happy places that just get better
and better. As you would expect, the staff are superb, the
rooms are comfortable, and we love the intimate, cosy
scale of the hotel.

- **OPEN:** Open all year, except Christmas
- **ROOMS:** 21 rooms, all en suite.
- **PRICE:** B&B from €120-€165 per room, €90 sin-
gle. €220-€240 per suite.

- **NOTES:** Visa, Access, Mastercard, Laser. Casey's
Bistro open lunch and dinner. Wheelchair access. Private
parking.

- **DIRECTIONS:**
Just outside Kenmare, on the right-hand side, at the
beginning of the Ring of Kerry, going towards Sneem.
GPS 5153.013N 935.4655W

CASTLEWOOD HOUSE

Helen & Brian Heaton
Dingle
County Kerry

☎ **+353 (0) 66-915 2788**
🖰 **www.castlewooddingle.com**
✉ **castlewoodhouse@eircom.net**

Helen and Brian's Castlewood House offers one of the finest breakfasts served anywhere in Ireland. And everything else here is just as perfect.

Castlewood is the sort of destination that Irish tourism needs In abundance. Brian and Helen run the house like the utter professionals they are, playing to their strengths, in particular creating a breakfast offer that is one of the very best in the country, executed with a stunning precision that gladdens the heart every morning. But the Heatons also make sure that despite being so busy – and they enjoyed another fine year in 2011, despite everything going on with the Irish and European economies – that they have time to chat, to offer local knowledge, to make sure that you are in the know, to make sure that you have what you need, even if you aren't entirely sure just what it is that you need. Style; comfort; service. Yes, you get all these at Castlewood but, above all, there is an intimacy about staying in a house like Castlewood which means that you feel you are right at the centre of the action, even if you are actually at the water's edge of Dingle Bay. It's a house that is a hub for hospitality, and for good times.

● **OPEN:** Feb-Dec. Open over New Year.
● **ROOMS:** 12 rooms, all en suite.
● **PRICE:** B&B from €39-€75

● **NOTES:** Visa, Access, Mastercard, Laser.
No dinner, but plenty of local restaurants within walking distance.
Wheelchair access.

● **DIRECTIONS:**
From Dingle take R559 towards Slea Head river. House is just 5 minutes' walk from marina and aquarium.
GPS 52.141311 -10.286142

EMLAGH HOUSE

Marion & Grainne Kavanagh
Dingle
County Kerry

- **+353 (0) 66-915 2345**
- **www.emlaghhouse.com**
- **info@emlaghhouse.com**

With elegant self-catering accommodation complementing the legendary stylishness of the house, Emlagh has it all.

Emlagh House has been in our *Bridgestone 100 Best Places to Stay* book ever since Grainne and Marian first opened their doors, which says all you need to know about this Dingle landmark. Emlagh is distinguished by good taste, good taste that is restrained, despite being undeniably expensive. Its signature is both that pervasive luxury, and also the sort of genuine hospitality that offers you a cup of tea and some superb home baking the very second that you walk in the door. Grainne and Marian work hard, and mother and daughter have that easy, confident, calm Kerry style of hospitality that puts you at your ease from the second you arrive. Most recently, they have opened superb self-catering accommodation, Water's Edge House, for those who want to make a Dingle holiday into a major family stay-over. The same exacting standards of housekeeping and attention to detail that characterise Emlagh are evident here: Water's Edge is sumptuous accommodation, with each apartment sleeping six.

- **OPEN:** Mar-Oct
- **ROOMS:** 10 rooms
- **PRICE:** B&B €70-€110 per person sharing, €40 single supplement

- **NOTES:** Visa, Access, Mastercard, Amex, Laser. No dinner. One room fully wheelchair accessible. Private car park. No facilities for children under 8yrs.

- **DIRECTIONS:**
Upon arriving in Dingle, take the first exit from the roundabout and Emlagh House is the first on left.
GPS 52.135119 -10.267133

HEATON'S HOUSE & RESTAURANT

Nuala & Cameron Heaton
The Wood, Dingle, County Kerry
🕿 **+353 (0) 66-915 2288**
🖰 **www.heatonsdingle.com**
🖂 **heatons@iol.ie**

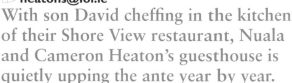

With son David cheffing in the kitchen of their Shore View restaurant, Nuala and Cameron Heaton's guesthouse is quietly upping the ante year by year.

Bridgestone Guide editor Caroline Byrne perfectly captured the singular element that makes Heaton's special, when she wrote that 'Cameron and Nuala kept a constant presence should we ever have needed anything, and any request was instantly obliged'. That's the secret of Heaton's, and what makes it one of the best destinations in Dingle. A fine, modern, comfortable house, a short walk from the bustle of the town and with fine views out over the bay, it's a house where the owners go the extra mile for their guests, preparing the most sublime breakfasts, and with the added bonus of David Heaton, a chef who has earned considerable experience in many of Ireland's best restaurants before returning home, rattling the pans in their Shore View restaurant. Mr Heaton's cooking concentrates largely, and wisely, on seafood, and his food has a summery, colourful disposition, allied to a very professional execution, and it makes for just the sort of thing you want to enjoy in Dingle, in just the right sort of house.

● **OPEN:** all year, except Dec-Feb. Open New Year.
● **ROOMS:** 16 rooms
● **PRICE:** €40-€65 per person, €46-€75 deluxe room, €54-€85 junior suite.

● **NOTES:**
Visa, Mastercard, Laser. Wheelchair access. Children welcome

● **DIRECTIONS:**
Overlooking the Harbour, just down from the Marina, near the roundabout in the centre of Dingle.
GPS 52.140594 -10.113581

85

HOTEL EUROPE

Michael Brennan
Fossa, Killarney
County Kerry
📞 **+353 (0) 64-667 1300**
🖥 **www.theeurope.com**
📧 **reservations@theeurope.com**

The team at the Hotel Europe work hard, determined to make every guest feel very special indeed. It makes for a sublime, luxurious Killarney getaway.

During the winter of 2011-12, The Europe will close in order to facilitate the second phase of their bedroom refurbishment, which will bring the Golfside rooms up to the standard of the Lakeside rooms. And that, let us assure you, is quite some standard: the luxury levels in the Europe are quite something, and their work over the last few years has brought this mighty hotel into the modern world with a bang. But, as Eamon Barrett has pointed out, such luxury would be empty without the appropriate levels of commitment and service to animate it, and here the Europe comes good: 'The staff are excellent... and there is a sense that, whatever your request, the Europe will be able to fulfill it'.

We have mentioned before two especially superlative elements of the Europe, the spa and pool, which are all their own work, and the views across the lake from the hotel, which are the work of Mother Nature, at her very best. Get a taste of these, and you'll fall in love with Killarney.

- **OPEN:** Apr-Oct
- **ROOMS:** 187 rooms and suites, all en suite.
- **PRICE:** B&B from €110 per person sharing

- **NOTES:** All major cards accepted. Full disabled facilities. Espa Spa, swimming pool, tennis court, horse riding, fishing and many other activities available. Dining options include cafe, bar, lounge service and restaurant.

- **DIRECTIONS:**
Hotel is just outside city centre, take the N72, travelling in the direction of Killorglin you will see sign on left.
GPS 52.067033 -9.571089

THE KILLARNEY PARK HOTEL

Padraig & Janet Treacy
Kenmare Place, Killarney
County Kerry
📱 **+353 (0) 64-663 5555**
🖰 **www.killarneyparkhotel.ie**
✉ **info@killarneyparkhotel.ie**

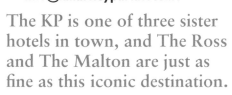

The KP is one of three sister
hotels in town, and The Ross
and The Malton are just as
fine as this iconic destination.

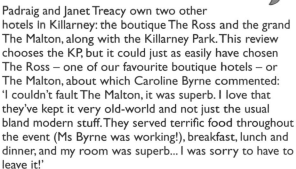

Padraig and Janet Treacy own two other
hotels in Killarney: the boutique The Ross and the grand
The Malton, along with the Killarney Park. This review
chooses the KP, but it could just as easily have chosen
The Ross – one of our favourite boutique hotels – or
The Malton, about which Caroline Byrne commented:
'I couldn't fault The Malton, it was superb. I love that
they've kept it very old-world and not just the usual
bland modern stuff. They served terrific food throughout
the event (Ms Byrne was working!), breakfast, lunch and
dinner, and my room was superb… I was sorry to have to
leave it!'
That's the Treacy signature: you will indeed be sorry to
leave these great temples of hospitality, temples of great
cooking, temples of comfort. The Treacys are obsessive
about getting the details right, and their staff follow them
to the letter. So each of the three hotels is different, but
they are united by a quest for excellence that is inspiring
and uplifting. The stars of Killarney.

- ● **OPEN:** All year, except Christmas
- ● **ROOMS:** 68 rooms
- ● **PRICE:** €250-€450 per room and suites

- ● **NOTES:** Visa, Mastercard, Amex, Laser. Restaurant &
Bar, Dinner €65. Children welcome. Full disabled access.
Swimming pool, spa.

- ● **DIRECTIONS:**
At 1st roundabout in Killarney (coming from Cork), take
1st exit for town centre. At 2nd roundabout take 2nd
exit and at 3rd roundabout take 1st exit.
GPS 52.0647 -9.5142

QC'S

Kate & Andrew Cooke
Cahersiveen, Ring of Kerry
County Kerry
- **+353 (0) 66-947 2244**
- **www.qcbara.com**
- **andrew@qcbar.com**

The five rooms in Kate and Andrew's QC's are a design triumph and the coolest getaway for 2012.

The five rooms in Kate and Andrew Cooke's restaurant with rooms, Q.C's, are the grooviest in all of Kerry. Killarney's The Ross comes close when it comes to style, but the use of colour here, the shocks of the throws and the headboards against the calm colours of the walls and the wood, interplayed with the control of light through shutters and Velux windows, is an utter triumph. You don't just want to stay in these rooms, you want to possess them, such is their astute luxury, their beyond-good finishing, their sense of escape. One of the secrets of their success may be that the rooms and furnishings are slightly larger-than-normal-life – there is space for lying, lounging, bathing, sleeping, dreaming, sharing breakfast in the room. God dammit, you can even stretch out and do your pilates and tai chi. So, we want to walk the Kerry Way around Cahersiveen, then return here each evening for baths and then a scrummy dinner of ace seafood in the restaurant. The coolest escape of 2012, no doubt about it.

- **OPEN:** All year, open Mon-Sun Easter-Oct, open weekends off season
- **ROOMS:** Five rooms, all en suite
- **PRICE:** €90 per room

- **NOTES:** Visa, Mastercard, Laser. Restaurant open lunch & dinner Easter-Oct, weekends only off season, Dinner €45. Wheelchair access.

- **DIRECTIONS:**
In the centre of Cahersiveen, which is on the Ring of Kerry.
GPS 51 56.753 North, 10 13.620 West

THE ROSS

Ciara Treacy
Town Centre, Killarney
County Kerry

📞 **+353 (0) 64-663 1855**
🖰 **www.theross.ie**
📧 **info@theross.ie**

Ciara Treacy is carrying on the Treacy family's mantle of distinguished hospitality in the almost impossibly hip The Ross, one of the great boutique hotels.

A new generation of the Treacy dynasty are taking up the reins at the family's iconic Killarney destinations. Ciara Treacy is now running the show in the super-stylish The Ross, the hotel where her grandmother first established the Treacy reputation as hoteliers par excellence, a tradition continued by her dad, Padraig, who runs both The Killarney Park and The Malton, but who served his time here in the centre of town. The Treacy signature is the art of being ahead of the curve, so The Ross not only has the slickest style in town, but also has the best cocktails, an area where Irish hotel bars have lagged behind the international trend to hire talented mixologists to give their bar an identity. So, a strawberry daiquiri for Mrs McKenna and a whiskey sour for Mr McKenna and then downstairs for dinner in Cellar One, where the cooking is as colourful and hip as the hotel's singular design ethos – chicken schnitzel with pesto; cod with soy mustard; Kerry beef with tomato and chorizo ragout. Impossibly cool.

- ● **OPEN:** All year, except Christmas
- ● **ROOMS:** 29 rooms and suites
- ● **PRICE:** B&B €160-€220 per room and suite

- ● **NOTES:**
All major credit cards accepted. Restaurant open for breakfast & dinner. Bar lunch. Wheelchair access. Private car parking. Leisure facilities of the Killarney Park Hotel.

- ● **DIRECTIONS:**
In the centre of Killarney, just round the corner from the main high street, beside the church.
GPS 52.05782 -9.50811

SHELBURNE LODGE

Tom & Maura Foley O'Connell
Killowen, Cork Road, Kenmare
County Kerry

- +353 (0) 64-664 1013
- www.shelburnelodge.com
- shelburnekenmare@eircom.net

For fifty years, Maura Foley has been the shining star of the food and hospitality culture of Kenmare.

Back in 1961, Maura Foley opened a cake shop in Kenmare. She didn't have a mixer. In 1991, she opened Packie's restaurant. In the mid 1990's, she began to renovate and develop Shelburne Lodge, which first appeared in the Bridgestone Guides in 1997. Has any other Irish person had such a major impact on the food culture of an Irish town? The answer, we would say, is: no. Mrs Foley's standards have set the template for Kenmare for more than half a century. Whilst many consider Myrtle Allen of Ballymaloe House to be the originator of contemporary Irish cooking, opening up in 1964, Mrs Foley actually was there a few years before. Her achievement is immense: a most distinguished cook, a most distinguished hostess, a most distinguished restaurateur. And Shelburne stands as testament to all her gifts, a most beautiful house characterised by fabulous comfort and design, characterised by great cooking, characterised by spontaneous generosity. She's the one, she's the one and only one.

- ● **OPEN:** Mar-mid Dec
- ● **ROOMS:** Seven rooms, all en suite
- ● **PRICE:** €100-€160 per room. Single €80

● **NOTES:**
Visa, Mastercard, Laser.
No restaurant (good restaurants locally). Enclosed car parking. No wheelchair access. Low season special rates available. Children welcome, high chair, cot.

● **DIRECTIONS:**
300m from the centre of Kenmare, across from the golf course on the Cork road.

BALLYOGAN HOUSE

Robert & Fran Durie
Graiguenamanagh
County Kilkenny
📞 **+ 353 (0) 59-9725969**
🖱 **www.ballyoganhouse.com**
📧 **info@ballyoganhouse.com**

A beautiful house, run with genial expertise by Robert and Fran Durie, Ballyogan benefits from owners who are real authorities on the region.

By the banks of the River Barrow, Ballyogan is such a pretty house, so comfortable in its place, so well sited, so well maintained. 'The level of hospitality had me smiling all the way: beautiful house and lovely people', says Bridgestone editor Eamon Barrett of his encounter with this genial gem in the heart of one of Ireland's most beautiful areas, the Barrow Valley, in and around Graiguenamanagh. The Duries are superb hosts, people who know everything about the area and what is going on there. They have restored Ballyogan with perfect grace and suitability, directing everything towards a welcoming comfort that makes you feel at home, just as some hot tea and cake, and superb breakfasts, will also mean you won't want to leave. It's not just the house that is in perfect order, mind you: the rolling lawns and mature trees seem as if they too have been arranged with benign care, and gazing out at them from the conservatory is a sublime, calm delight. This is just the place from which to explore this beautiful, quiet region.

● **OPEN:** 1 Apr-31 Oct
● **ROOMS:** two twin rooms, one double and one family room
● **PRICE:** B&B €46-€50 per person sharing, single €58-€60

● **NOTES:** Visa, Mastercard, Laser. No wheelchair access. Dinner on request, €35-€40.

● **DIRECTIONS:**
From Graiguenamanagh take R705 New Ross rd for 4.5km. House is signposted on left from this road. GPS 53.509444 -6.940083

THE INN @ BALLILOGUE CLOCHÁN

Pat McCarthy, Ballilogue, The Rower Inistioge, County Kilkenny
📞 + 353 (0) 51-423857
🖱 www.ballilogueclochan.com
✉ enquiry@ballilogueclochan.com

Pat McCarthy's make-over at The Inn is a wow! Both vernacular and cutting-edge, the style is pure bliss.

Something new

'Nestled away on a boreen near The Rower in South Kilkenny, Pat McCarthy's farmhouse renovation is a star' says Eamon Barrett. A collection of old outbuildings have had a magic wand – and not a small amount of money – waved over them to create a series of beautiful rooms both vernacular and cutting edge. Exposed stone walls, old dressers and mismatched crockery are mixed with power showers, Barcelona chairs, original art and lovely light fittings. Manager, Mark, offers tea and lemon cake on arrival and later, while we slip into pretending that we live here and read books in one of the lounges, brings local cheese and oat biscuits to go with a nice bottle of Sauvignon Blanc. The surroundings are sylvan, the garden is perfect, good taste abounds. Next morning the breakfast doesn't miss a beat: fresh orange juice, homemade brown bread, light as a feather pancakes with Greek yoghurt, blueberries and honey, cinnamon French toast with maple syrup. Value is excellent and The Inn is simply a stunning achievement.

● **OPEN:** all year, apart from Christmas and New Year
● **ROOMS:** six rooms, all en suite
● **PRICE:** B&B €110-€245 per person sharing, single €85-€140

● **NOTES:** Visa, Mastercard, Laser. Wheelchair access. WiFi. Mature gardens. Not suitable for children. Self-catering options.

● **DIRECTIONS:**
12km south of Inistioge in the direction of New Ross (R700). Look for a sharp right turn and sign 10km beyond Inistioge. GPS 52.43.11 -6.99.21

MOUNT JULIET

William Kirby
Thomastown
County Kilkenny
📞 **+ 353 (0) 56-777 3000**
🖱 **www.mountjuliet.ie**
💌 **info@mountjuliet.ie**

Nobody is trying harder to be their best than the crew at beautiful Mount Juliet: these guys are up for it!

Something new

Nothing cheers a critic more than a crew who are determinedly working to be their best. That, after all, is what we mean by 'The Best In Ireland' – people determined to do their best, be their best, achieve their best. And in Mount Juliet, manager William Kirby and his cheffing trio – Cormac Rowe, Ken Harker and John Kelly – are determined to give us the best that they've got. In the past, we had simply sidelined Mount Juliet as a plush hideaway for golfers with too much money. And it is plush, and grand. And there are people in golf sweaters – at breakfast time! Ouch! But that doesn't matter, because what counts here is a place determined to reach out to its local community through sourcing the best Kilkenny ingredients, a place that is ingenious and creative and very, very beautiful, and where the staff work extra hard. 'A breath of fresh air and fresh thinking', said the 'Times. They also have more grey squirrels than we have ever seen in our lives.

● **OPEN:** all year, including Christmas and New Year. Weekends only off season.
● **ROOMS:** 31 rooms, all en suite, 10 lodges and 16 club house rooms
● **PRICE:** B&B €139-€159 per room, with supplements for suites.

● **NOTES:** All major cards accepted. Wheelchair access. Equestrian Centre, Leisure Centre, Golf Course.

● **DIRECTIONS:**
Leave the M9 on exit 9. Drive through Stoneyford and look for their sign. GPS Locate Code RC3-58-KV7

IVYLEIGH HOUSE
Dinah & Jerry Campion
Bank Place, Portlaoise
County Laois
📞 **+353 (0) 57-862 2081**
🖱 **www.ivyleigh.com**
📧 **info@ivyleigh.com**

Ivyleigh is the star of Portlaoise, thanks to Dinah Campion's authoritative understanding of just how to mix past and present in one lovely house.

Tradition is one of those terms the Irish aren't really comfortable with. Talk about traditional food, for instance, and they imagine some fossilised culinary relic of times past, rather than a contemporary food culture infused with knowledge of the past. Similarly, when it comes to design, the Irish reckon you have either got to be modern, or live in an ancient mausoleum. Dinah Campion's lovely house, Ivyleigh, proves that this dichotomy is false. The style here is traditional, but is infused with a modern eye that emphasises lightness and brightness. The cooking, at breakfast, is traditional, which is to say it takes the best of the past and shares it with the best of the present – delicious cooking, but modern and light, well-sourced and cooked with exacting precision. Mrs Campion, in this way, creates a masterly synthesis in Ivyleigh, making for a place of good-mannered civility, understated charm, an alliance of the personal with the professional that is terrifically successful. Ivyleigh House is the star of Portlaoise.

● **OPEN:** All year, except Christmas
● **ROOMS:** Six rooms, all en suite
● **PRICE:** B&B €40-€75 pps. Single room €55-€85

● **NOTES:** Visa, Mastercard. No dinner.
No wheelchair access.
Off street car parking. available
Children over 8 years welcome.

● **DIRECTIONS:**
In Portlaoise, follow the sign for multi-storey car park.
At car park entrance there is a sign with directions for
Ivyleigh House.

ROUNDWOOD HOUSE

Hannah & Paddy Flynn
Mountrath
County Laois

📞 **+353 (0) 57-873 2120**
🖥 **www.roundwoodhouse.com**
📧 **info@roundwoodhouse.com**

One of those great country houses
that seem to exist in its own universe
and its own time, Hannah and Paddy's
Roundwood House is simply a peach.

'It's still a family environment and our guests seem to
like that', Hannah Kennan told Mary Leland in *The Irish
Times* in early 2011. Thank heavens for family continuity,
for new generations who are happily carrying on the
pioneering work of their parents. Can you just imagine
what would have happened to Roundwood if it had
fallen into the hands of some 'developer'. The family
environment would have been the first victim of such a
change – even though it explains everything about this
gorgeous house – quickly followed by a lavish spend
that would have obliterated the very thing that makes
Roundwood so lovable – the fact that it isn't polished
and perfect, but has, instead, a wabi sabi quality to it.
Wabi sabi Roundwood? Well, yes, Roundwood expresses
the perfection of imperfection, the beauty of something
aged, something organic. And now, blessed with the
energy of Hannah, and her husband Paddy, Roundwood
is perfectly poised for the future, the family environment
intact, ready for the next 300 years.

● **OPEN:** All year, except Christmas
● **ROOMS:** 10 rooms, all with private bathrooms
● **PRICE:** €60-€80 per person sharing. Single supple-
ment €15

● **NOTES:** All major cards accepted. Dinner at 8pm,
€35-€50, communal table. Book by noon. No wheelchair access. Recommended for children.

● **DIRECTIONS:**
Turn right at traffic lights in Mountrath for Ballyfin, then
left onto R440. Travel for 5km on the R440.
GPS 53.024 -7.527

THE COURTHOUSE

Piero & Sandra Melis
Main Street, Kinlough
County Leitrim

☏ **+353 (0) 71-984 2391**
⌂ **www.thecourthouserest.com**
✉ **thecourthouserest@eircom.net**

Piero Melis runs a special place to eat and stay in lovely little Kinlough, a place where everything chimes sweet and true, instinctive and generous.

Piero Melis' Courthouse has made it into the sister volume to this book, the *Bridgestone 100 Best Restaurants in Ireland 2012*, for the first time. His cooking has always been great, but, like every aspect of this happy restaurant with rooms, it has recently simply gotten better and better. The explanation for such steady improvement is simple: Mr Melis is dedicated, devoted, talented, and supremely hard working. He will be in the kitchen last thing at night, working away, working away and, then, first thing in the morning he will be there to make sure your breakfast is as perfect as your dinner was – and, of course, it will be just as perfect. We also love the fact that everything here – the restaurant, the rooms, the service, the wines – is modest, apposite, simple and genuine. Our most recent stay here was part of a Leitrim weekend that took in a course at the Organic Centre, and it was one of the best weekends we have ever enjoyed. Next time, it's going to be surfing, then back to the Courthouse for dinner and bed.

● **OPEN:** All year except Christmas. Thur-Sun only Oct-Feb
● **ROOMS:** Four rooms
● **PRICE:** B&B €37 per person sharing, €42 single

● **NOTES:** Visa, Mastercard, Laser. Wheelchair access. Restaurant opens for Dinner, 6.30pm-9.30pm, ('till 10pm high summer), and Sun lunch, noon-2.30pm. No wheelchair access to rooms.

● **DIRECTIONS:**
On the main street in Kinlough, opposite the post office. GPS 54.450 -8.285

THE MUSTARD SEED

Daniel Mullane
Echo Lodge, Ballingarry
County Limerick
📞 **+353 (0) 69-68508**
🖱 **www.mustardseed.ie**
✉ **mustard@indigo.ie**

Dan Mullane's country house
and Mustard Seed restau-
rant has been making people
happy for 25 years.

We have described Dan Mullane as 'a poet of the aesthetic world, a man whose grasp of design, comfort and
style is matched by few others In Ireland'. That's true
– only people like Paddy Foyle and Ken Buggy have the
sort of crazy, meticulous, inspired eye that Mr Mullane
has when it comes to shaping a room, a house, a garden.
His brilliance makes Echo Lodge, where his Mustard
Seed restaurant is housed, into one of the most pleas-
ing houses to stay in anywhere in Ireland. But being a
master of design is meaningless without the hospitality
that truly animates a room, a restaurant, a house, and,
guess what? Dan Mullane is as inspired a host, as he is a
designer. In fact, he is even better as a host than he is as
a designer. For more than 25 years he has been greeting,
meeting, and making welcome, and he does it today with
the freshness, the zest, the spontaneous wit and natural
charm, that first marked him out as someone special
all those years ago. A special guy, in a special house. Just
don't miss it.

- **OPEN:** All year, except last 2 weeks in Jan & Xmas
- **ROOMS:** 18 rooms, including three suites
- **PRICE:** €65-€160 per person

- **NOTES:** Visa, Mastercard, Access. Dinner €62.
Wheelchair access. Box room special rate €65 per
person, sharing. Early bird menu options. Resident Thai
masseuse. Pet friendly.

- **DIRECTIONS:**
Take the Killarney road from Adare, 500m until you
reach first turning off to the left, signed for Ballingarry.
GPS 52.474672 -8.864692

NUMBER ONE PERY SQUARE

Patricia Coughlan
1 Pery Square, The Georgian Quarter
Limerick City, County Limerick
📞 **+353 (0) 61-402402**
🖱 www.oneperysquare.com
📧 info@oneperysquare.com

*One Pery Square is the star
of Limerick city, the centre of
both Limerick hospitality and
creative Limerick cooking.*

Patricia Coughlan talks about attempting to create a 'home from home' experience at One Pery Square. If only our homes had rooms as meticulously styled and furnished as these! If only we lived in a smart Georgian townhouse! If only our homes had a chic spa, and a wine shop, and a chef like Alan Burns in the kitchen! If only! Staying at OPS can be quite momentous: our friend Joe McNamee, writing in *The Irish Examiner,* described OPS as 'my new favourite hotel in the world', and said that his room was 'the first hotel room I've liked in years'. That's the kind of magic Ms Coughlan is weaving here, an intoxicating mix of style, comfort and seriously fine cooking, in a space that you very quickly want to make your own. In that sense, One Pery Square is indeed 'home from home': you feel that you own it, and there is none of that alienating sense of distance which other boutique hotels can't manage to overcome. It's a marvellous confection, and One Pery Square is a place where everything works.

● **OPEN:** All year, except 24-28 Dec
● **ROOMS:** 20 rooms, all en suite

● **PRICE:** €67.50-€97.50 per person sharing

● **NOTES:** All major credit cards accepted.
Dinner available in Brasserie.
Wheelchair access.
Spa and wine shop.
Valet car parking.

● **DIRECTIONS:**
On the corner of Pery Square and Barrington Street.

VIEWMOUNT HOUSE

Beryl & James Kearney
Dublin Road, Longford
County Longford
☎ **+353 (0) 43-334 1919**
🖰 **www.viewmounthouse.com**
✉ **info@viewmounthouse.com**

Fantastic cooking at breakfast,
and outstanding food from Gary
O'Hanlon in the restaurant, makes
Viewmount Longford's brightest star.

Viewmount is the place that has put Longford on the culinary map. Thanks to Beryl and James Kearney's hospitality, and Gary O'Hanlon's dynamic cooking, Longford has gotten the destination it has so long needed. Viewmount itself is a place with two identities: there is the original house, dating from the 1740's, surrounded by peaceful gardens with especially beautiful, mature trees, and this is where James and Beryl Kearney look after you. The second identity, then, is the modern, hip VM restaurant where every Longford food lover – and many from much further afield – come to eat delicious, inventive cooking from Mr O'Hanlon, cooking which exploits the richness and variety that can be sourced from local artisans, hunted down by Mr O'Hanlon himself. The McKennas all ate superbly when at Viewmount, both at dinner, and with a brilliant breakfast cooked by James, served in one of the atmospheric rooms of the house. It's a mighty one-two, one of the best double-acts in Irish cooking and hospitality.

- **OPEN:** Open all year
- **ROOMS:** 12 rooms, all en suite
- **PRICE:** B&B €55-€65 per person

- **NOTES:** Visa, Mastercard, Laser, American Express. VM Restaurant, Wed-Sat 6.30pm-9.30pm & Sun lunch 1pm-4pm. Lunch €29 Dinner €53. Wheelchair access.

- **DIRECTIONS:**
From Longford town, take R393 to Ardagh. After 1km take right turn onto slip road and then follow signs to the house.
GPS 53.72246 -7.77105

GHAN HOUSE

Paul Carroll
Carlingford
County Louth
📞 **+353 (0) 42-937 3682**
🖱 **www.ghanhouse.com**
✉ **ghanhouse@eircom.net**

Paul Carroll is one of the unsung masterminds of modern Irish hospitality. He and his team in Ghan House are always striving to do better, every day.

'As invigorated as ever!', writes Paul Carroll. There are a lot of people in Irish hospitality that would love to be able to say that about their work. So, what is Mr Carroll's secret? What is it about running the lovely Ghan House that so invigorates him? Doing a better job, every day, is the answer. This crew never rest on their efforts, or even their laurels. They are always searching for ways to get better, like introducing a great value midweek tasting menu, so that more people can get a chance to sample Robert Read's fine, fine cooking – 18-hour Kettyle short ribs of beef; belly of Fermanagh pork with Carlingford crab; wild Wicklow venison with beetroot jelly; lemon tart with frozen Limencello yogurt. With the kitchen powering ahead, Mr Carroll just makes sure to take care of the beautiful gardens, and the beautiful house, and in Ghan House he has created a shrine to hospitality in Carlingford, one of the most beautiful villages in the country. Stay and eat for a day or two, and get invigorated yourself!

● **OPEN:** All year, except Christmas & New Year
● **ROOMS:** 12 bedrooms, all en suite
● **PRICE:** €99-€125 per person sharing, includes dinner

● **NOTES:** Visa, Mastercard, Access, Amex. Restaurant open six nights. No wheelchair access. Midweek and weekend breaks. Cookery school. Horse riding.

● **DIRECTIONS:**
First driveway on left after 50kph sign on entering Carlingford. 85km from Dublin, 69km from Belfast.
GPS 54.040278 -6.184167

BERVIE

John & Elizabeth Barrett
The Strand, Keel, Achill
County Mayo

☎ **+353 (0) 98-43114**
🖰 **www.bervie-guesthouse-achill.com**
📧 **info@bervie-guesthouse-achill.com**

For eighty years, John and Elizabeth's Bervie has been a beacon of hospitality – and philosophy – for visitors to Achill. Don't forget the surfboard.

Philosophy. Don't you just love a house where the first category on their website – even before you get to the accommodation and the food – is 'philosophy'. Ah, little Bervie, an old coastguard station dating from 1932, a place where you step from the garden through a little wicket gate, and there you are on the beach at Keel strand. If this is philosophy, then it is epicureanism, pure and simple, the simple and modest life, the untroubled soul, flecked with sea salt and sand and sunshine. Bervie makes you a child all over again.

Elizabeth cooks whilst John pulls the corks, and the food, like the philosophy, is simple and true, the foods of the area cooked in the way that suits them best. Don't miss the unique Achill lamb, which enjoys a distinctive pré-salé taste that deserves to have its own geographical label, for it is as distinctive as Connemara lamb, but more saline, more succulent. The food, the comfort, the calm rooms, all chime as sweetly as good philosophy. Bervie creates a synthesis for your soul.

● **OPEN:** Easter-Nov
● **ROOMS:** 14 rooms, all en-suite
● **PRICE:** B&B €50-€65 per person sharing. Weekly, full board rates also available.

● **NOTES:** Visa, Mastercard, Laser.
Dinner available in their restaurant.
Dinner €45. Wine list.
Musical evenings, adjacent beach.

● **DIRECTIONS:**
In the village of Keel on Achill Island.
GPS 53.972686 -10.084319

ICE HOUSE

Dara Cruise
The Quay, Ballina
County Mayo
☎ **+353 (0) 96-23500**
🖱 **www.theicehouse.ie**
✉ **chill@theicehouse.ie**

The Ice House is visually stunning, at every point, with a breathtaking location on the River Moy, to the luxe rooms, and the stylish food on the plate.

Set hard by the banks of the River Moy, just a few minutes' walk from Ballina town, the Ice House is visually stunning when you glimpse it first: a piece of rigorous, angular design that is every bit as jaw-dropping as the views down-river at this idyllic location. Inside this beautiful temple of stylishness, manager Dara Cruise has always had a great team working alongside him, and good service has always been a feature of highly motivated, welcoming staff. Donegal man Kwangi Chan heads up the kitchen team, and working with good west coast ingredients such as the local Clarke's salmon from Ballina, Bluebell Fall's goat's cheese from County Clare, Dromoland estate venison, Glasan Farm beef, and leaves from the local Blas Glas organic farm, he fashions smart, polished plates, and the care lavished on everything from breakfast through to their smart bar bites – Clarke's smoked haddock fish fingers in poppy seed beer batter with hand-cut chips: wow! – shows a very determined team who are working hard.

● **OPEN:** All year, except 25-27 Dec
● **ROOMS:** 32 bedrooms, all en suite
● **PRICE:** B&B €160-€190 per person

● **NOTES:**
Visa, Mastercard, Laser. Wheelchair access
Dinner served nightly from 6pm, lunch and bar menu also available. Booking required. Pet friendly.

● **DIRECTIONS:**
From Ballina follow road past Dunnes Stores. Take first exit on mini roundabout. Travel over bridge, take left turn onto N59. Take first left to Quay Road.

KNOCKRANNY HOUSE HOTEL

Adrian & Ger Noonan
Westport
County Mayo
☎ +353 (0) 98-28600
🖰 www.khh.ie
🖂 info@khh.ie

Seamus Commons' food has
put Knockranny House Hotel
on the map, and the hotel is
firing on all cylinders.

Owners Adrian and Ger Noonan and head chef Seamus
Commons will have to build an extension to the Knockranny House Hotel if they keep on collecting awards at
the rate they have been hauling them in over the last
two or three years. The most recent big gong was when
chef, Mary Ryan, won the Eurotoques young chef award
for 2011, always a significant award, and proof that the
talent in Knockranny goes right through the kitchen
team. Whilst Seamus Commons' cooking attracts most
attention to the hotel, it has to be said that everything
else here works just as well: service is excellent, the
housekeeping is meticulous, the spa is luxurious. But
the cooking really is something else, a hugely exciting
series of improvisations on fantastic ingredients that is
worth the acclaim, and then some. We tell the story in
the 100 Best Restaurants 2012 of how a bunch of stellar
European chefs were blown away by the Knockranny
cooking, and be assured that you will be blown away too.
A great destination, that's steadily becoming greater.

● **OPEN:** All year
● **ROOMS:** 97 rooms, all en suite

● **PRICE:** B&B and Dinner from €75

● **NOTES:** Visa, Mastercard, Amex.
Restaurant open dinner, €54 Bar Lunch.
Full disabled facilities.

● **DIRECTIONS:**
Off the Dublin/Castlebar Road, 10mins from
Westport town centre.
GPS 53.80306 -9.50806

MULRANNY PARK HOTEL

Dermot Madigan
Mulranny
County Mayo
📞 **+353 (0) 98-36 000**
🖰 **www.mulrannyparkhotel.ie**
✉ **info@mulrannyparkhotel.ie**

The Mulranny Park is one
of the best in the west, a
glorious resort hotel with
staff who revel in their work.

Teenage hoodie-wearers take their chosen garments
very seriously indeed. Selecting the right hoodie says a
great deal about places and things that teenagers consider cool. After Sam and PJ McKenna stayed with their
dad in the Mulranny Park, they wore their MP hoodies
with great pride, and it wasn't until some Electric Picnic
hoodies came along much later in the year that the MP
hoodies had to cede pole position. So, teenagers think
the Mulranny Park is cool, right? Dead right! They love
the pool, the games room, they love the Great Western
Greenway so they can cycle on bikes into Newport, they
love the breakfasts, they love the glam of the restaurant
and they love Ollie O'Regan's fantastic food. Above all,
they love the fact that the Mulranny feels like a real hotel, like a proper hotel, with a sense of history. Dermot
Madigan and his team are doing a fantastic job here, and
the attention to detail – from the brown bread to the
Curraun blue trout – is exacting. A tip-top address on
tip-top form.

- **OPEN:** All year
- **ROOMS:** 41 rooms, all en suite, 20 apartments
- **PRICE:** B&B €60-€89 per person sharing.

- **NOTES:** Visa, Mastercard, Laser, Amex.
Nephin Restaurant open dinner, €37.50 Waterfront Bar
menu served noon-9pm. Wheelchair access.

- **DIRECTIONS:**
From Westport, take the N59 through Newport. Continue on the R311 to Mulranny village. Pass through the
village and the hotel is on your right.
GPS 53 54.334, 9 46.908

HOTEL MANAGERS

1

ADRIAAN BARTELS
CLIFF HOUSE HOTEL

2

DERMOT BRENNAN
BROOK LANE

3

RONNIE COUNIHAN
RENVYLE HOUSE

4

NEIL GRANT
WEST CORK HOTEL

5

SIMON HADEN
GREGAN'S CASTLE

6

NEIL LUCEY
GOUGANE BARRA HOTEL

7

DERMOT MADIGAN
MULRANNY PARK

8

ANNE McKIERNAN
BROOK'S HOTEL

9

PATRICK O'FLAHERTY
BALLYNAHINCH CASTLE

10

FIONA TEEHAN
PEMBROKE HOUSE

STELLA MARIS

Frances Kelly & Terence McSweeney
Ballycastle
County Mayo
📞 **+353 (0) 96-43322**
🖱 **www.StellaMarisIreland.com**
📧 **info@StellaMarisIreland.com**

Frances & Terence's stellar house has been one of the catalysts, and one of the leading lights, of Mayo's renaissance.

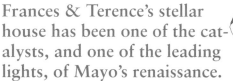

When we first wrote about Terence McSweeney and Frances Kelly's country house, Stella Maris, way back in 2003 just after they opened, we predicted it would be one of the stars of the next ten years. Everything a great country house needed was in situ, most of all the dynamism of this talented couple. For once – once! – we were right. Stella Maris is today recognised as one of the best places to eat and stay in Ireland, and it has gained that reputation thanks to the devotion and discipline of this couple, a pair of fastidious hotel keepers. Ms Kelly's cooking, in particular, is all her own, and modestly and precisely executed in every detail. It is food that comforts while it delights, country cooking ennobled by classy ingredients, cooking that has the most complete confidence of all: the confidence to be simple, the confidence to let the food be itself, and to taste of itself. Years after you first eat Ms Kelly's food, the memories of the precise flavours and textures will come back to you, happy memories of a happy place.

- **OPEN:** Easter-early Oct
- **ROOMS:** 11 rooms
- **PRICE:** B&B €95-€120 per person sharing

- **NOTES:** Visa, Mastercard. Wheelchair access. Limited ability to accommodate young children. A la carte dinner served 7pm-9pm.

- **DIRECTIONS:**
Go down the hill from Ballycastle, and the Stella Maris is signposted from here. Turn right, it's on the Pier Road, overlooking the sea.
GPS 54.298484 -9.388575

WESTPORT PLAZA

John Clesham
Castlebar Street, Westport
County Mayo
📞 **+353 (0) 98-51166**
🖱 **www.westportplazahotel.ie**
📧 **info@westportplazahotel.ie**

Joe and Anne Corcoran offer two superbly run hotels in Westport: the Plaza and the Castlecourt. Both are distinguished by superb service.

Joe and Anne Corcoran's hotel is one of those destinations where things are always done correctly. The greeting, the service, the cooking, the housekeeping all sync beautifully here, and the professionalism of the staff gladdens the heart. The Corcorans have a very clear vision of creating and keeping a happy workforce as the means by which you create happy guests in an hotel, and they have made this simple, sympathetic philosophy work, both in the Plaza itself and in its larger, adjacent sister hotel, the Castlecourt. There is such an evident sense of commitment from the staff here that it strikes you the very second you walk through the door – nothing is too much trouble, anything you need to know they know already, or will find out for you. This is just the spirit you want to discover when staying in a resort hotel in a holiday town like pretty Westport, and manager John Clesham and his crew come up trumps. Nice cooking in Restaurant Merlot – Angus beef with horseradish mash; Newport lamb with piperade – completes the picture.

- **OPEN:** All year including Christmas
- **ROOMS:** 87 rooms, all en suite
- **PRICE:** B&B €49-€160 per person sharing

- **NOTES:** Visa, Mastercard, Laser, Amex.
Wheelchair access.
Full restaurant facilities in the Restaurant Merlot and Plaza Bar

- **DIRECTIONS:**
As you approach the town from Castlebar, the hotel is at the first set of traffic lights on your right-hand side.
GPS 53.801261 -9.518608

COOPERSHILL HOUSE

Simon O'Hara
Riverstown
County Sligo
📞 **+353 (0) 71-916 5108**
🖥 **www.coopershill.com**
✉ **reservations@coopershill.com**

An 18th-century eco-house?
Believe it or not, but that
is exactly what Simon and
Christine's Coopershill is.

There is something about Coopershill that is artfully smart. You could take one look at this big 18th-century pile and feel sorry for the owners – the maintenance! the heating bills! the roof! the damp! But your sympathies would be misplaced, for the house is actually uber-green, and has major environmental awards patting them on the back for their wood-burning stove, their rain-water harvesting, their wetland drainage system. They have a tidy business selling their superb venison, another award-winning venture. And when you stay and eat dinner, they can virtually count how many metres many of the ingredients you will be enjoying will have travelled to reach your plate: 50 metres for the vegetables? 200 metres for the venison? Some of it will be even closer. Country houses used to be worlds unto themselves, and Simon and Christine run Coopershill in just that fashion: self-sufficient people in a supremely self-sufficient place. It's a gorgeous house, and Christine's cooking is amongst the best you will find.

● **OPEN:** Apr-Oct B&B, Private groups, min 12, all year
● **ROOMS:** Eight rooms, all en suite
● **PRICE:** B&B €99-€122 per person sharing

● **NOTES:** Visa, Mastercard, Laser. Children welcome tennis court, gardens, croquet, walks. Pets can overnight in owner's car. No disabled facilities. Afternoon tea €5, for residents, Picnics €15 pp, light lunch €15, Dinner €49

● **DIRECTIONS:**
On N4, 19km south east of Sligo. At Drumfin cross-roads follow signs.
GPS 54.1381 -8.4154

INCH HOUSE

Mairin Byrne
Thurles
County Tipperary
☎ **+353 (0) 504-51261/51348**
🖱 **www.inchhouse.ie**
📭 **mairin@inchhouse.ie**

The Egans are a pivotal part of the burgeoning Tipperary food culture, and they have been doing the good thing for almost a quarter of a century.

The Egan family are amongst the most dynamic of the food pioneers who together have created the impressive wave of artisans and restaurateurs that now characterise the county. John and Nora Egan opened their house to guests in 1989, adding the restaurant five years later, so there is nearly a quarter century of service from the family to their community. Whilst Nora Egan has ceded the day-to-day running of the house to her daughter, Mairin, she has developed a parallel career as the creator of Inch House black pudding, a wonderful artisan pudding, which won a bronze award at the Concours International du Meilleur Boudin competition in France in 2011. Mairin, meanwhile, runs this fine house and restaurant with the confidence that comes of family experience, and both the house and the restaurant are places of quiet excellence. Inch is a wonderfully comfortable place to stay, and a wonderfully comfortable place to have dinner, enjoying real Tipperary tastes and treats.

- **OPEN:** All year, except Christmas
- **ROOMS:** Five rooms, all en suite
- **PRICE:** €45-€55 per person sharing, Single supplement €10

- **NOTES:**
Visa, Master, Laser, Dinner 6.30pm-9.30pm Tue-Sat. No wheelchair access.

- **DIRECTIONS:**
6.4km from Thurles on the Nenagh Road, R498. Turn off at the Thurles exit on the main M8 road.
GPS 52.7211183 -7.92173333

THE OLD CONVENT

Dermot & Christine Gannon
Clogheen
County Tipperary

☎ **+353 (0) 52-746 5565**
🖰 www.theoldconvent.ie
✉ info@theoldconvent.ie

Dermot Gannon's cooking in
The Old Convent in Clogheen
is nothing less than the Golden
Mean of the Golden Vale.

In his last report on Dermot and Christine
Gannon's The Old Convent, Eamon Barrett signed off
by saying: 'And finally, a lovely goodbye'. After all that
had gone before, which was basically two extraordinary
meals – the tasting menu dinner and the scrumptious
breakfast, and a day relaxing and enjoying the comforts
of this fine, fine house – Mr and Mrs Gannon even manage 'A lovely goodbye'. Ahhh. Doesn't that do your heart
good? But it's true: everything in The Old Convent is
heartfelt – the welcome, the care, the cooking, even the
goodbye, are all genuine and sincere. This explains how
the house has been such a success, because after leaving
the first thing you want to do is to return. And you want
to return to enjoy again that extraordinary cooking, an
eight-course symphony that pays tribute to the great
artisans from whom Mr Gannon sources his ingredients.
His food is the Golden Mean of the Golden Vale, a thing
of rare beauty perfectly in symmetry, in proportion and
in harmony.

● **OPEN:** All year, except Christmas-end Jan. Weekends only off season.
● **ROOMS:** Seven rooms, all en suite
● **PRICE:** B&B €80-€95 per person sharing, €40
single supplement

● **NOTES:**
Visa, Mastercard, Laser. Dinner in restaurant Thu-Sat,
one sitting, 8-course tasting menu, €65. No wheelchair
access. Private car parking. Not suitable for children.

● **DIRECTIONS:**
On the R668 Cahir to Lismore road.

CLIFF HOUSE HOTEL

Adriaan Bartels
Ardmore
County Waterford
☎ **+353 (0) 24-87800**
🖱 **www.thecliffhousehotel.com**
✉ **info@thecliffhousehotel.com**

Who's the guy sitting in the Jacuzzi in the pouring rain? That's Eamon Barrett. He's, em, with the *Bridgestone Guides.*

You can take Eamon Barrett to The Cliff House anytime. Here's his latest: 'Consistent excellence - that is the elusive standard that so many five-star hotels fail to achieve, but at Cliff House consistent excellence is what you get. Before you even get out of the car there is someone to greet you with a bit of chat and take your bags. The rooms are universally impressive, regardless of whether you're in the most basic room or glamming it up in the duplex Terrace Suites, and there's no escaping the setting, on the cliffside overlooking the stunning Ardmore Bay. Of course, Martin Kajuiter's food is a huge component of Cliff House, as you might expect. What you might not expect is how much fun it is to try to hit a golf ball onto the hotel's floating green out in the bay. Or to leave the heated swimming pool and take a dip in the rock pool beneath the hotel. Or sit in the Jacuzzi in the pouring rain. Such fun is all the more enjoyable because, despite the hotel's status, it is not in the least bit stuffy.'

- **OPEN:** all year except Christmas
- **ROOMS:** 39 rooms
- **PRICE:** B&B from €200 per room

- **NOTES:** All major cards accepted. Wheelchair access. Restaurant open for dinner, €67.50-€90. Bar serves food noon-9pm. Loc8 code YSB-80-TR9

- **DIRECTIONS:**
From the N25 turn onto the R673 signposted Ardmore. Once in Ardmore take the Middle Road to the hotel.
GPS 51.948614 -7.715078

GLASHA FARMHOUSE

Olive O'Gorman
Ballymacarbry
County Waterford
📞 **+353 (0) 52-613 6108**
🖥 **www.glashafarmhouse.com**
✉ **glasha@eircom.net**

Olive O'Gorman has fashioned a brilliant makeover of the dining room in Glasha farmhouse, a house where things only ever get better and better.

Most of the people who stay at Glasha seem to be frequent visitors, returning one more time for Olive O'Gorman's great hospitality, returning one more time to this beautiful area, so beloved of hillwalkers and hikers. But, no matter how often you have stayed, you will still be blown away by the transformation of the Glasha dining room when you sit down to dinner on your next visit. What was once a comfortable but domestic space is now a super-cool room of poised elegance, with a patio door out onto the walled courtyard. It's a stunning makeover but, to tell you the truth, it's not a bit surprising that Olive should have pulled off such a stylish coup. She is a determined and driven woman, someone who always wants to transcend her best, and her cooking and her house show her determination in action. So, after a big afternoon hike in the hills, peel off the Osprey backpack and ditch the Mendls, and bring on the Comeragh lamb with rosemary, the striploin with creamed mushrooms, and the good red wine.

- **OPEN:** Jan-Dec
- **ROOMS:** Six rooms, all en suite
- **PRICE:** B&B €50-€60 per person sharing. Single supplement €60-€70

- **NOTES:** Visa, Mastercard, Laser. Dinner 8.30pm €45. Children over 12 years welcome. Secure parking. Wheelchair access.

- **DIRECTIONS:**
Well signposted, off the R671 between Clonmel and Dungarvan. 3km from Ballymacarbry.
GPS 52.276058 -7.759528

BY THE COAST

1
**BERVIE
COUNTY MAYO**

2
**CLIFF HOUSE HOTEL
COUNTY WATERFORD**

3
**DOLPHIN BEACH
COUNTY GALWAY**

4
**HERON'S REST
COUNTY GALWAY**

5
**KELLY'S RESORT HOTEL
COUNTY WEXFORD**

6
**MOUNT VERNON
COUNTY CLARE**

7
**NEWTOWN HOUSE
COUNTY CORK**

8
**MULRANNY PARK HOTEL
COUNTY MAYO**

9
**THE QUAY HOUSE
COUNTY GALWAY**

10
**THE SALTY DOG HOTEL
NORTHERN IRELAND**

RICHMOND HOUSE

Paul & Claire Deevy
Cappoquin
County Waterford
☎ **+353 (0) 58-54278**
🖱 **www.richmondhouse.net**
✉ **info@richmondhouse.net**

Paul and Claire Deevy are master and mistress of one of the great Waterford treasures, Richmond House.

The McKennas had all driven from West Cork to Cappoquin for the launch of Esther Barron's book on the history of Barron's bakery, and when we arrived at Richmond, we sat down in the drawing room and had fresh, warm scones and handmade jam and a pot of tea. The fire blazed away, the comfort was as palpable as the sense of welcome. Was there ever such a happy bunch of travellers, so happy to have arrived at their destination, in such a happy place as Richmond House? Out of such precious, unexpected moments, moments of thoughtfulness and generosity, spring a lifetime's worth of happy recollections, and that is exactly what Paul and Claire Deevy specialise in, in this lovely country house. They are elemental, thoughtful people. They and their team look after you, and make sure you have everything you could possibly need, from the tea and scones on arrival to Paul's lovely country cooking at dinner and then their delicious breakfasts to set you up for the day. Richmond is a special place, a place where time takes its time.

● **OPEN:** All year except Christmas
● **ROOMS:** Nine rooms
● **PRICE:** from €60 per person sharing, Single supplement €20

● **NOTES:**
All major cards accepted. Restaurant open for dinner only, Mon-Sun (closed on Sun in winter), €53
Private parking. Children welcome, babysitting, toys.

● **DIRECTIONS:**
Just outside Cappoquin, the house is well signposted.
GPS 52.139261 -7.846708

THE TANNERY TOWNHOUSE

Paul & Máire Flynn
10 Quay Street, Dungarvan
County Waterford
📱 **+353 (0) 58-45420**
🖰 **www.tannery.ie**
📩 **info@tannery.ie**

Maire Flynn brings a powerful sense of aesthetics to the Tannery Townhouses, the complement to Paul Flynn's cooking.

Talk of The Tannery tends inevitably to focus on Paul Flynn, chef, television star, cookery teacher, food writer. Mr Flynn's fame is well-deserved, because he is one of the foremost Irish chefs of his generation, with a style of cooking that is all his own. And, he is seriously funny. But just as important to The Tannery, and the two gorgeous Tannery Townhouses, is Maire Flynn, who tends not to get written about, other than being mentioned as being Mr Flynn's partner. Mrs Flynn is funny, smart and droll, and she is a pivotal part of this singular operation, not merely in terms of efficiency and aesthetics, where her fingerprints are everywhere, but in terms of the no-nonsense, down-to-earth lack of pretension that is the hallmark of this brilliant operation. For a person who largely stays in the background, she is actually larger-than-life, an aspect of her character she reveals most through social media, where she lets her star shine. So, behind every great woman, there is a great man.

- ● **OPEN:** All year, except late January
- ● **ROOMS:** 14 rooms, all en suite
- ● **PRICE:** from €50 per person sharing, Single €70

- ● **NOTES:** Visa, Mastercard, Laser, Amex. Tannery Restaurant is open for dinner Tue-Sat, 6pm-9.30pm. Lunch Fri & Sun.
Cookery School.

● **DIRECTIONS:**
20m from The Tannery Restaurant, beside the Old Market House building.
GPS 52.08864 -7.61677

LOUGH BISHOP HOUSE

Helen & Christopher Kelly
Derrynagarra, Colinstown
County Westmeath
📞 **+ 353 (0) 44-9661313**
🖱 **www.loughbishophouse.com**
📧 **chkelly@eircom.net**

Lough Bishop House is a
place where even the cows
have sweet, suggestive names.
The real Irish agri-turismo.

Lily. Patricia. Gwen. Hilda. Viola. Sweetheart. Go on,
have a guess? Who are we talking about? The newest
Sugababes? The latest Girls Aloud? No, it's something
much more important than that. We are talking about
the Irish Moiled cows and heifers that you might meet
at Helen and Christopher's idyllic Lough Bishop House.
Along with Irish Draught horses, Helen and Chris breed
Irish Moiled cattle and, along with Jersey and Kerry
cows, they are surely the most beautiful things munching
in a field near to you. That's the thing about the Kellys:
everything they do has an aesthetic edge, so the cows
aren't just gorgeous, they even have sweet, Edwardian-
style names – a cow named Hilda! This is typical of
Lough Bishop, a gorgeous place, and the ultimate Irish
agri-turismo. Lough Bishop is a true demonstration farm,
for it demonstrates how farming can be a cultural and
aesthetic practice, and how a farm can be an idyll, a place
where time is brought back to agricultural time. There's
nowhere like Lough Bishop.

● **OPEN:** All year, except Christmas and New Year
● **ROOMS:** Three rooms, including family room
● **PRICE:** B&B €55 per person sharing, €10 single
supplement

● **NOTES:** No credit cards. Dinner, 7pm, (book before
noon), €30. Working farm. No wheelchair access.

● **DIRECTIONS:**
From Castlepollard take the R394 Mullingar road, turn
left opposite Whitehall School and Church, L5738.
2km up that road on the right-hand side.
GPS 53.6344166 -7.26471666

WINEPORT LODGE

Jane English & Ray Byrne
Glassan, Athlone
County Westmeath
📱 +353 (0) 90-643 9010
🖥 www.wineport.ie
✉ lodge@wineport.ie

A Babymoon? Actually, it's a Teenagemoon we need, and Wineport is just the right place to get that r'n'r!

Babymoon. No, we hadn't heard it either, until we saw that Babymoon breaks are one of the special getaways that Ray and Jane offer in The Wineport. A Babymoon is a final chance for a couple to getaway together before junior arrives, and reshapes your life in ways you had never imagined. We're not sure if there is such a thing as a Teenagemoon, but we would sure be game ball for one and, now that we have mentioned it, we are sure that Ray Byrne will invent just such a package. Mr Byrne is not just one of the great hoteliers of his generation, but he is also one of the most creative, inventive and disciplined. We have followed his career in our books since long before Wineport was ever created, and he has always been the most perspicacious, forward-looking operator. In Wineport, he marshals a superb team, and so everything here is as good as it can be, as good as they can make it, not least the superb modern Irish cooking of chef Cathal Moran which is amongst the best cooking to be found in the Midlands.

- **OPEN:** All year
- **ROOMS:** 29 rooms
- **PRICE:** B&B from €79 per person sharing. Upgrades and weekend breaks also available.

- **NOTES:** All major cards accepted. Restaurant serves dinner, à la carte 4-course menu, approx €50. Wheelchair access.

- **DIRECTIONS:**
At Athlone, take the Longford exit off Dublin/Galway rd, fork left at the Dog & Duck. Lodge is 1.5km further on, on the left. GPS 53.465578 -7.883470

KELLY'S RESORT HOTEL

Bill Kelly
Rosslare
County Wexford

☏ **+353 (0) 53-913 2114**
🖱 **www.kellys.ie**
✉ **info@kellys.ie**

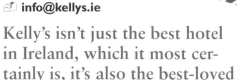

Kelly's isn't just the best hotel in Ireland, which it most certainly is, it's also the best-loved hotel in Ireland, for sure.

'I am a host to everyone who stays', Bill Kelly told an interviewer a few years back. 'I like to talk to them, to greet them and welcome them. It's the way we've always done it.'

Talk to them, greet them, welcome them. That's a trinity of imperatives ready to stand alongside Michael Pollan's great mantra about food: 'Eat food. Not too much. Mainly plants.' Like Pollan's aphoristic haiku, Bill Kelly's few words reveal exactly why and how Kelly's Hotel is the best hotel in Ireland, and the best-loved hotel in Ireland: people welcome you, they greet you, they talk to you. That's hospitality, that's hotel keeping, and Bill Kelly has no peers as an hotelier. His family-run hotel is one of the glories of modern Ireland, a destination with a unique aesthetic, a place where a talented team do their best, every day. The cooking, the art collection, the wines, the comfort, all take place within the context of an hotel where you are greeted, made welcome and chatted to. So simple, so profound, so perfect.

● **OPEN:** Feb-early Dec
● **ROOMS:** 118 rooms, all en suite
● **PRICE:** Spring/autumn: weekend €290pp; 5-day midweek from €535pp; Summer: 7-day rate from €950pp. Shorter breaks available. All full board.

● **NOTES:** All major cards accepted. All rates include full board. La Marine restaurant also comes recommended. Wheelchair access. Every facility for children & babies.

● **DIRECTIONS:**
Clearly signposted in Rosslare.

McMENAMIN'S

Seamus & Kay McMenamin
6 Glena Terrace
Spawell Road, Wexford
📞 + 353 (0) 53-914 6442
🖥 **www.wexford-bedandbreakfast.com**
📧 **info@wexford-bedandbreakfast.com**

Seamus and Kay McMenamin push the right buttons, and it knocks their customers for six, thanks to tender loving care, and amazing breakfasts.

Some people know just how to push the right buttons. Seamus and Kay McMenamin are two of those people. When they opened their B&B they brought to it a lifetime's worth of experience in the hospitality business, and it shows. Other hosts are generous amateurs, but the McMenamins are generous professionals. They can read your mind. They know that you really crave baked lamb's kidneys cooked in sherry for your breakfast, but would be too shy to ask for them. So, they chalk it up on the blackboard, and then Seamus will persuade you that baked lamb's kidneys in sherry is what you really feel like this morning. And you will agree, and that extra special breakfast will linger in your memory for years as a symbol of the perfect indulgence in the perfect moment on a perfect morning at McMenamin's. Creating that special moment is what Seamus and Kay do, and their cosy, classic house is the perfect backdrop for one of the best B&B experiences you can enjoy in Ireland. They push the right buttons, every time.

● **OPEN:** Mar-Dec
● **ROOMS:** Four rooms

● **PRICE:** B&B from €45-€50 per person sharing

● **NOTES:**
Visa, Mastercard, Laser.
No dinner.
Wheelchair access.

● **DIRECTIONS:**
In the centre of Wexford, opposite the County Hall.

MONART

Liam Griffin
The Still, Enniscorthy
County Wexford
☏ **+353 (0) 53-923 8999**
🖱 **www.monart.ie**
✉ **reservations@monart.ie**

'Monart is the antithesis of Celtic Tiger excess', says Eamon Barrett. Beautiful house, great staff, a magical escape.

Monart got it right when it opened, and continues to get its alliance of relaxation and invigoration just right, whilst improving with age. 'Monart confounds your expectations, and therein lies its success', says Eamon Barrett. 'It's a glitzy, glamorous place, a modern extension added onto a lovely old building, with electric gates to enter - all of these things make you expect the worst of Celtic Tiger 'We have built it and therefore it will be brilliant' excess. In fact, nothing could be further from the truth. At its core are wonderful staff, who love hospitality to their fingertips - if you've been before they know what room you were in, they welcome you back, and they mean it. The architecture is wonderful, curved wings spanning out into the woods from the main building and as the grounds have matured the calmness that is inherent at Monart has just increased. Everything is kept spick and span and even if you are not the type of person who likes to spend a weekend in a robe you will still find much to enjoy at Monart.'

● **OPEN:** All year, except Christmas
● **ROOMS:** 70 rooms
● **PRICE:** €95-€250 per person sharing, €695 upwards for suite, depending on dates and availability, single supplement €40

● **NOTES:** Visa, Master, Amex. Dinner, €39.50. Wheelchair access. Over 18 yrs only. Spa open 9am-9pm. No functions. D+ B&B rates quoted, see website.

● **DIRECTIONS:**
Just off the N11 road to Gorey. See map on website.
GPS 52.513889 -6.613889

BALLYKNOCKEN HOUSE

Catherine Fulvio
Glenealy, Ashford
County Wicklow

📞 **+353 (0) 404-44627**
🖱 **www.ballyknocken.com**
✉ **info@ballyknocken.com**

Television and books and cover stories don't alter Catherine Fulvio one iota: this girl is a real Wicklow woman.

'I'm a real Wicklow woman', Catherine Fulvio told the writer Pól O Conghaile. Indeed she is. The married name may be Italian, but her maiden name is Catherine Byrne and what she does in Ballyknocken is simply continuing the family business, running a B&B and restaurant – and a cookery school – which dates back to 1969, when her mum first took in guests. We have known Mrs Fulvio since long before she took over at Ballyknocken, and aside from her work ethic, her skills and her astounding efficiency, she has always impressed us as a person who knows, first and foremost, who she is: she is a real Wicklow woman. Her cooking shows this: it's gutsy food that she likes to cook, suitable for folk who have had a busy day doing good work, and there is both purity and simplicity in it, along with the generosity that is an integral, defining, part of her work. Breakfasts are as delicious as dinner, with all the meals bringing the true tastes of Wicklow to the table. Ballyknocken is truly a great destination, the real thing.

- **OPEN:** mid Feb-mid Dec
- **ROOMS:** Seven rooms
- **PRICE:** From €49-€59 per person sharing.

- **NOTES:** Visa, Mastercard. Dinner, Fri, Sat €45. No wheelchair access.
Cookery school.

- **DIRECTIONS:**
From Dublin, head south to Ashford (on N11), then turn right after Chester Beatty pub. Continue for 5km and the house is on the right.
GPS 52.9769666 -6.14308333

THE BROOK LODGE INN

Evan, Eoin & Bernard Doyle
Macreddin Village, Aughrim
County Wicklow
☎ **+353 (0) 402-36444**
🖱 **www.brooklodge.com**
✉ **brooklodge@macreddin.ie**

The Brook Lodge has been the most dynamically creative hotel in Ireland over the last decade, and it keeps getting better.

Evan Doyle is the most dedicated and creative hotelier of his generation, and the achievement of himself and his crew in the Brook Lodge is one of the glories of modern Irish hospitality. Everything in this extraordinary hotel is aimed at offering an authentic experience, an original experience. When the travel writer Catherine Mack stayed here, the only word that she found adequate to describe the experience of the hotel and the spa and the food and the wines and the world that is Brook Lodge was: 'Wild!'. 'It just works in certain circumstances, when superlatives won't do the trick', wrote Ms Mack. Tell us about it! We have spent more than a decade exhausting the superlatives in an attempt to describe what happens in this amazing complex, when all we should have been saying was 'Wild!' So, if you want your mind to be opened, and blown apart, by the most authentic experience of food, hospitality and nature imaginable, then the Brook Lodge will do just that for you. 'Wild!' in every way.

● **OPEN:** All year, including Christmas
● **ROOMS:** 90 rooms and suites
● **PRICE:** B&B from €55 per person sharing, single supplement €40. Also web offers.

● **NOTES:** All major cards accepted. Two restaurants, pub, market and bakery. Secure car parking. Reservations essential. Limited wheelchair access.

● **DIRECTIONS:**
From Rathdrum, take R753 to Aughrim (12km). In Aughrim turn right at church and follow signs. Do not use Sat Nav. GPS 52.8796666 -6.3315

FOR WALKERS

1

**FORTVIEW HOUSE
THE SHEEP'S HEAD WAY**

2

**GHAN HOUSE
THE TAIN WAY**

3

**GLASHA FARMHOUSE
COMERAGH MOUNTAINS**

4

**GREGAN'S CASTLE
BURREN HILL WALKS**

5

**LINSFORT CASTLE
MAMORE TO DUNREE**

6

**MARLAGH LODGE
SLEMISH MOUNTAIN**

7

**MULRANNY PARK
GREAT WESTERN GREENWAY**

8

**QC'S
THE KERRY WAY**

9

**ROUNDWOOD HOUSE
SLIEVE BLOOM WAY**

10

**STEP HOUSE HOTEL
THE BARROW WAY**

Northern Ireland

BEECH HILL HOUSE HOTEL

Patsey O'Kane
Londonderry
County Londonderry
📞 **+44 (0) 28-7134 9279**
🖱 **www.beech-hill.com**
✉ **info@beech-hill.com**

Patsey O'Kane is one of the greatest hoteliers, and she is one of the most important figures, in Northern Ireland's unique culture of hospitality.

We are great admirers of Patsey O'Kane, an hotelier who is one of the great figures of Northern Irish hospitality. Ms O'Kane incarnates that true hospitality which the people of Northern Ireland exude, and she frames it within the rigour of acute professionalism, and within the lovely aesthetic of the Beech Hill House itself. Ms O'Kane is to Northern hospitality what Myrtle Allen is to Southern hospitality: an original, a person of true conviction, a shining, modest star. What makes the Beech Hill special is simple, and utterly fundamental: everyone in the hotel over-delivers, everyone is always trying to do their best, to make sure that every detail is done right, done as well as it can be. That is the art of hotel keeping, that is the very essence of the art we look for in the Bridgestone Guides, and Ms O'Kane is mistress of that art and practices that art every day in her work in this beautiful, early 18th-century house. Beech Hill is two miles from Derry but, truthfully, it is a place unto itself, a palace of hospitality. Give this woman a peerage.

● **OPEN:** All year, except 24-25 Dec
● **ROOMS:** 27 rooms and suites
● **PRICE:** B&B £60-£117.50 per person sharing, £95-£105 single

● **NOTES:**
All major cards accepted. Ardmore Restaurant open for lunch and dinner. Wheelchair accessible.

● **DIRECTIONS:**
On the A6 direction in Londonderry, take the turning off at Faughan Bridge. Travel 1 mile to Ardmore Chapel, where you will see the hotel entrance on your left.

THE CARRIAGE HOUSE

Maureen Griffith
71 Main Street, Dundrum
County Down
📞 **+44 (0) 28-4375 1635**
🖱 **www.carriagehousedundrum.com**
✉️ **inbox@carriagehousedundrum.com**

'Thank you for all the delightful guests you have sent my way', says Maureen Griffith. Delightful guests, and the delightful Carriage House!

South County Down – drumlin country – is one of those areas of Ireland that will, someday soon, and deservedly, be discovered by folk from the Republic. Golfers know it, of course, but for walkers and nature lovers this area is something of a paradise, unspoilt.

The jewel of hospitality to match the jewel nature of the area is Maureen Griffith's Carriage House, in lovely Dundrum. A pioneering restaurateur – Mrs Griffith originally ran the Buck's Head Inn, today masterminded brilliantly by Alison and Michael Carruthers – before creating the ravishing visual palette that is the Carriage House. We use the term palette because everything here is painterly, and painterly perfect. Ms Griffith has the aesthete's eye, and the perfectionist's rigour, so the house and the garden and the cooking are all, equally, of a superb standard. Add in the mix of places to eat in the village, and Dundrum offers all you need for a superlative base. Mind you, after breakfast in the Carriage House, you may feel like doing not much at all...

● **OPEN:** All year
● **ROOMS:** Three rooms, all en suite
● **PRICE:** £75 double room, including breakfast, Single room £45

● **NOTES:** No credit cards. No dinner, but two excellent restaurants, adjacent to building. Storage for guests' bicycles. No wheelchair access, bedrooms on second floor. Postcode BT330LU. WiFi.

● **DIRECTIONS:**
Dundrum is on the main Belfast to Newcastle road (A24), and The Carriage House is in the centre of town.

DUFFERIN COACHING INN

Leontine Haines
Killyleagh
County Down
☎ +44 (0) 28-4482 1134
🖥 www.dufferincoachinginn.com
✉ info@dufferincoachinginn.com

Leontine Haines' Dufferin Coaching Inn is handsome, professional, polished and pretty, a great destination. All banks should become such B&Bs.

Leontine Haines got all the details right before opening her doors in this lovely, early 19th-century coaching house in pretty Killyleagh. Part of the building was formerly a bank but, unlike most Irish banks, Ms Haines actually knows how to run a business properly and professionally. The rooms and bathrooms are beautifully appointed, the towels are fluffy, the Bircher muesli at breakfast is as scrumptious as all the other homemade ingredients that comprise the feast that starts the day. Many guests choose to eat next door at the friendly Dufferin Arms, where the cooking is good, or at Balloo House where the brilliant Danny Millar cooks up a storm, with some of the most inventive cooking in Ireland. Leontine enjoyed another excellent year in 2011 as word spreads about this special house, a destination that is another feather in the cap of this lovely village in this lovely region. Wine buffs, by the way, shouldn't miss a visit to Jim Nicholson's stunning wine shop in nearby Crossgar, the most beautiful wine shop in Ireland.

● **OPEN:** All year
● **ROOMS:** Seven rooms, all en suite
● **PRICE:** B&B £65-£90 per room (£45-£65 for single occupancy)

● **NOTES:**
All major cards accepted.
No wheelchair access.

● **DIRECTIONS:**
Killyleagh is 16 miles, half an hour's drive, from Belfast, and the Inn is in the town centre, next to the Dufferin Arms.

MARLAGH LODGE

Robert & Rachel Thompson
71 Moorfields Road, Ballymena
County Antrim

☎ **+44 (0) 28-2563 1505**
🖰 **www.marlaghlodge.com**
📭 **info@marlaghlodge.com**

Exploring the Glens of Antrim? Then Marlagh Lodge, with its fab country cooking, is your destination.

When we were writing the text for the places to stay and eat for *The Irish Times* Great Drives app – you can get it at *www.irishtimes.com/mobile* – one of the drives created by Bob Montgomery was on the A43, around the Glen of Antrim. Well, that was an easy one to do, we said to ourselves: if you are up exploring the Glens, then you stay and eat at Marlagh Lodge. It is as simple as that. Starting from a near-ruin, and less than a decade ago, Robert and Rachel Thompson have resurrected, renovated and restored a stunningly beautiful house, with apposite period details in every room. What is equally stunning is Rachel's glorious cooking, with every dish both graceful and flavour-filled, carefully sourced and cooked, enjoyed in the William Morris-style room by candlelight, with a bottle of wine from James Nicholson's wine merchants to add to the pleasure. Could anything be nicer after a day driving through the Glens? No sir. Mrs Thompson is a true cook, with verve and style in every dish she prepares.

- ● **OPEN:** Open all year, except Christmas
- ● **ROOMS:** Three rooms, all en suite
- ● **PRICE:** B&B £50 per person

● **NOTES:**
Mastercard, Visa, Switch, Maestro. Dinner, 8pm £32.50 (book by noon). No wheelchair access.

● **DIRECTIONS:**
From the A36 to Larne, turn onto Rankinstown Road, and the driveway is immediately on your left.
GPS 54.846111 -6.226944

THE SALTY DOG HOTEL

Ashleigh & Hans Arthur
10-12 Seacliff Road
Bangor, County Down
☎ **+44 (0) 28-9127 0696**
🖰 **www.thesaltydoghotel.com**
📧 **info@thesaltydoghotel.com**

Has Bangor got what it takes to be the new Kinsale? If the town's restaurants work together, the answer is yes.

Something new

Is Bangor the new Kinsale? Jorris Minne, of *The Belfast Telegraph*, says that it is, citing the presence in the town of Coyle's, The Boathouse, Jeffers and Café Essence and, of course, the Salty Dog, where Derek Creagh has been cooking up a storm, and getting the 'Dog into our *100 Best Restaurants Guide*. Certainly, this is an impressive array of talent in the little seaside town, but the difference between Kinsale and Bangor is a simple one, and reveals a lesson that the Bangor restaurants can learn from. Kinsale restaurants are formidably well organised as a publicity machine, and have been so for nearly 40 years. If Bangor can get its act together, and restaurants and boutique hotels like The Salty Dog are exactly what the visitor ordered, then they can have a long, successful tenure pulling food lovers to the town for the next few decades. The mix of straight-ahead cooking and excellent rooms in this smart hotel is an example of how to do it right. Curiously, John McKenna used to eat rollmop herrings here, 40 years ago.

- **OPEN:** Open all year, except Christmas
- **ROOMS:** 15 rooms, all en suite
- **PRICE:** B&B £70-£95 per double room, £55-£65 single

- **NOTES:**
All major cards accepted.
The Salty Dog, Bridgestone recommended restaurant open lunch and dinner.
Wheelchair access.

- **DIRECTIONS:**
Overlooking the Marina at Bangor's seafront.

Other titles from Estragon Press ...

The companion volume to this book is:

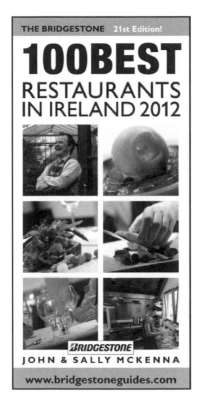

Every year the Bridgestone editors seek out those restaurants that offer the best cooking and the best service in Ireland. In this book you will find bustling city restaurants, and tiny single-room restaurants in the farthest flung corners of the country.

CONTACT THE BRIDGESTONE GUIDES:

We greatly appreciate receiving reports, e-mails and criticisms from readers, and would like to thank those who have written in the past, whose opinions are of enormous assistance to us when considering which 100 places finally make it into this book.

Our website has two contact forms - one to contact us, and the other to make recommendations.

We love hearing from you.

twitter

facebook

www.bridgestoneguides.com